Rekindling the Human Spirit

An Anthology of Hope, Courage and Inspiration

Cher Holton, Ph.D. & Bil Holton, Ph.D.
Editors

Featuring a Foreword Interview with
Jamie Valvano Howard
Remembering her father, Jim Valvano

Liberty Publishing Group
Egg Harbor • Frederick • Raleigh

This publication is designed to provide accurate and authoritative information in regard to the subject matter covered. It is sold with the understanding that the publisher is not engaged in rendering legal, accounting, or other professional service. From a Declaration of Principles jointly adopted by a Committee of the American Bar Association and a Committee of Publishers.

We gratefully acknowledge The V Foundation for permission to reprint photographs of Jim Valvano.

Clipart used with permission - © 2003 www.clipart.com
All other artwork/photos owned by artists, used with permission.

Publisher's Cataloging-in-Publication Data

Rekindling the Human Spirit
-- 1st ed.
    p. cm.
    ISBN 1-893095-20-7

Library of Congress Control Number: 2003104700

10   9   8   7   6   5   4   3   2   1

12/03

Dear Susan —
This was an opportunity for me
to achieve one of my dreams — to be
published — I hope these stories
help you through any difficult
times — & I hope those difficult
times are few!
            Love,
            Chris

In everyone's life, at some time, our inner
fire goes out. It is then burst into flame by
an encounter with another human being.
We should all be thankful for those people
who rekindle the inner spirit.
– Albert Schweitzer (1875 - 1965)

Table of Contents

Contents

Contents

Contents

A Note From the Editors ...

We are excited and proud to offer *Rekindling the Human Spirit: An Anthology of Hope, Courage and Inspiration*, at such an unprecedented time in our history. As a world, we have taken our first tentative steps into the challenges, uneasiness and global upheavals of the 21st Century. We are the heirs of all that has been attempted and accomplished, and shareholders in what we as humans can do to improve ourselves and the world in which we live. As responsible human beings, we have an obligation to let our lights shine so we can lead others through the darkness of despair and disappointment. That's exactly what the loving and capable contributors to this anthology have done. Their collective wisdom offers guidance and direction to light the way through troubled times.

In this rekindling anthology, we offer readers light from many lamps. We were honored to work with so many wonderful contributors, who inspired us with their material. All of the quotes, poems, anecdotes, illustrations, motivational passages and stories come from ordinary people who have extraordinary stories, talents, and advice to share. The material comes from human beings who are catalysts, encouragers, motivators and survivors. In fact, some of the most helpful and inspiring passages in this anthology come from the personal achievements, perseverance, and survivorship moments of people who have worked through incredible life challenges.

Selections were not made on the basis of a contributor's status, position, or literary credentials, but solely on the basis of inspirational impact. The poems and artwork of the children who contributed are just as powerful and meaningful as the stories, illustrations, quotes, and poems written by the adults. We believe the contents of *Rekindling the Human Spirit* will speak to your heart. There are selections for the worried, ailing and angry. There is advice for those who think life isn't fair, and guidance for those who refuse to bow to adversity – who fear or doubt the unknown. There are passages which praise the courage, resilience and tenacity of the human spirit. There are perspectives which assure the reader that life, with all its problems and frustrations, has meaning and purpose.

We are especially grateful to Jamie Valvano Howard, who saw the worth of this project and so graciously added her own thoughts, memories and wisdom to give readers a glimpse of one of the most extraordinary rekindlers of all time – her father, Jim Valvano.

We believe many people will be blessed for having read *Rekindling the Human Spirit*. We encourage you to keep a copy nearby so you can turn to it for inspiration when you most need it. Give a copy to someone important in your life. And never miss an opportunity to do some little thing to rekindle the spirit of each person whose life you touch.

- Cher & Bil Holton, Editors

"Don't Give Up! Don't Ever Give Up!"®
The Legacy of Jim Valvano
An intimate interview with Jim Valvano's daughter, Jamie Valvano Howard

No one epitomizes the spirit of rekindling the human spirit more than Jim Valvano, most remembered as the North Carolina State University basketball coach who, in 1983, convinced his underdog Wolfpack team they could overpower Houston in the NCAA Championship game. The team staged one of the biggest upsets in NCAA history, and were forever labeled 'The Cardiac Pack.'

Equally as powerful is the image of a gravely ill Jim Valvano, inspiring millions with his unforgettable televised speech, accepting the Arthur Ashe Award for Courage at ESPN's inaugural ESPY Awards in 1993. Jim Valvano was truly a man of courage and inspiration, and provided hope for others.

As this book is going to press, the sports world is celebrating the 20th anniversary of the Wolfpack's amazing NCAA victory, and remembering their famous inspirational coach. It is fitting that we have this opportunity to get an inside look at Jim Valvano – the coach, the motivator, the father, the man. In this exclusive interview with his middle daughter, Jamie Valvano Howard, we get a glimpse into what made Jim Valvano tick, and how he lived his passion of rekindling the human spirit in everything he did.

As we conducted this interview, it was clear from the beginning that Jamie Valvano Howard is her father's daughter. She is gracious, enthusiastic and openly passionate about the legacy her father left the world!

Liberty Publishing Group: Jamie, thank you so much for agreeing to endorse our anthology, *Rekindling the Human Spirit,* by sharing some stories about your dad, Jim Valvano ... one of the greatest rekindlers of all time.

Jamie Valvano Howard: I am so honored to have this opportunity to celebrate his life, and remember the amazing impact he had – and continues to have – on so many people. And I am thrilled to be a part of this anthology. If there was ever a time when spirits needed rekindling, it is now. You are right on target with this wonderful book, and I sincerely hope a lot of people read it.

LPG: Thank you! Jamie, when I think about the word Rekindling, one of the first images to flash in my mind is your dad. So it's perfect to have you kick off the book with memories of him. I'd really like to just let you share your favorite stories with us. I remember hearing you speak once, and you said your father was your hero.

JVH: That's so true. He taught me a lot about how to live life to its fullest. Do you know that when he was 17 years old, he took out a note card and wrote down all the things he wanted to accomplish in his professional life? He wanted to play basketball in high school and college, become an assistant coach, then a head coach at the college level. He wanted to win a big game in Madison Square Garden, and then cut down the nets after winning a National Championship. Big dreams for a skinny Italian kid from New York! By the way, do you notice the theme? Basketball was his love!

LPG: He certainly made a name for himself in the sports world!

JVH: He was such an amazing influence – not just in the sports world, but with everyone he met. He made everyone feel valued, like they mattered to him, even if it was just a brief encounter. He gave so much of himself to everything he did. When I think of my dad, I think of him as a man of action, a man of the people, a man of courage.

LPG: That sounds like a good 3-point speech – or should I say 3-point play?

JVH: It sure does! I guess the action part is a good place to start. My dad once commented, "There are 86,400 seconds in a day. It's up to you to decide what to do with them." Well, Jim Valvano decided he would do it all! He refused to limit himself to the typical boundaries of one profession. He was possessed by life and all the opportunities it had to offer! For example, after reaching the highest level of success as a basketball coach, he won an award as a TV commentator at ABC and ESPN. He authored three books (one is a cookbook!), gave hundreds of motivational speeches, hosted TV and radio shows, and showcased his wonderful sense of humor on *The Tonight Show, David Letterman,* and *The Cosby Show.*

LPG: He was one busy man! We think of Jim Valvano as a real motivator. Perhaps his greatest motivational success was in 1983, when he convinced the N.C. State basketball team they could win the NCAA Championship. So tell us, how did he do it?

JVH: He was so proud of that team! He really believed that his job, as coach, was to make those young men believe they were winners. At the end of practice, he would bring out a ladder and place it under the net. Then he would take out a pair of scissors and encourage all the team members to scream and shout as if they had just won the National Championship! One by one, each player would climb up the ladder as the rest of the team cheered, and cut a piece of the net. Then my father would climb up and cut the last piece, look out at an imaginary celebrating crowd, and wave the remnants of that net over his head with an expression of pure joy! After doing this all season, the team started to envision themselves actually cutting down the net, and they began to dream about making it a reality.

LPG: Wow! That gives me huge goose bumps! What a great example of truly visualizing and believing in your dreams. I know that anyone who watched that final game will remember forever the vision of your father encircling the court in search of someone to hug!

JVH: Yes! My dad was a real hugger! In fact, he once said, "To fully understand how close-knit a family I grew up in, we hugged, kissed, touched and said 'I love you' so much we should have been X-rated."

LPG: Jim Valvano was truly on top of the world after the '83 Championship. He really connected with everyone.

JVH: I am still amazed at the impact he had on people. To this day, folks come up to me and share their favorite *Jimmy V* story. My dad would love that. He was truly a man of the people. Well, look at that … we've transitioned right into the second point!

LPG: Swish! Now that we're on the second point, tell me –why do you think Jim Valvano was such a 'man of the people' – such an inspiration to so many others?

JVH: Jim Valvano could not have existed without people! He had a deep love for humanity  … the world was his team! I think his secret was his passion for people, for life. It showed in everything he did. He had an uncanny way of connecting with people, quickly and deeply. He never met a stranger! He not only helped his players believe they were winners, he wanted everyone to believe they were winners! People gave him his energy.

LPG: Since we're focusing on rekindling, may we talk about the painful period your father experienced when, as Coach and Athletic Director, he was involved in an investigation that ended with him leaving N.C. State University?

JVH: That was a very difficult time for my dad – for all of us. But I agree it is important to talk about, so people can see how he handled the tough times. That's part of what characterized my dad. He lost his dream job that he had been working toward and building since he was 17 years old. And it wasn't done quietly. But here's what I remember from that dark period. Nobody was calling. There were no requests for speeches, job interviews, appearances. My dad had to go inward, and with the love and support of his family, he had to rekindle his own inner spirit. I remember he was at home a lot more than my sisters and I could ever remember. He played golf, and bought stuff on the Home Shopping Network! But whenever any of us started feeling low about the situation, or began criticizing the way it was being handled, he would pull out one of his favorite poems. (He was an English major in college, and always shared his love of literature with us.) The poem was *If*, by Rudyard Kipling. The part that really hit home were the lines that said:

If you can meet with Triumph and Disaster
And treat those two impostors just the same;
If you can bear to hear the truth you've spoken
Twisted by knaves to make a trap for fools,
Or watch the things you gave your life to broken,
And stoop and build 'em up with worn-out tools ...

Then he'd stop and say that's what he was doing, rebuilding with his worn-out tools. We really thought he would slow down after this experience, but no, not Jim Valvano! He signed with ABC/ESPN as Basketball Commentator/Analyst, and the next year (January, '92) won the Cable ACE Award! He never did anything halfway.

LPG: Wow! He rekindled his career when others would have just given up. What an inspiration.

JVH: Yes, but his biggest challenge – and his biggest legacy – was yet to come. And this is when we discovered he was a such a man of courage. In June of 1992, he was diagnosed with Metastatic Adenocarcinoma – terminal cancer. For most people, that would signal a time to pull inward, wrap up life's details, and wait for the end. But this is when Jim Valvano's true spirit really began to shine. He took out that old note card and wrote down one final dream – find a cure for cancer. With only a notepad and a pencil, he began planning a

Foundation. To the end, his thoughts and actions were focused on helping and inspiring others.

I remember him saying he didn't want to lose his hair, because he wanted to be able to continue working as Commentator on ESPN. We were surprised he'd even want to remain in that role, with his weakness and pain. But he said, "If people see me on TV every week, they will know there's hope. I want to show them you can defeat any obstacles life throws at you." He literally shared his personal fight against cancer with the world.

LPG: And he succeeded in creating that Foundation, didn't he?

JVH: He certainly did! It is really amazing. There was no seed money – none! He got the support of ESPN, who allowed him to announce the formation of The V Foundation for Cancer Research at the inaugural ESPY's in '93.

You know, it is unbelievable. His doctors didn't even want him to go to that ceremony. But Dad was determined to be there. He was extremely sick, tumors all over his body, in a wheelchair. He had no prepared speech, and we all figured he would accept the award, say thank-you, and leave the stage. But no! After being helped to the stage, he gave the speech of his lifetime! He knew this was his chance to inspire others, and he managed to dig down deep into his reserves and pull out the energy to mesmerize the crowd.

LPG: Talk about rekindling! Jim Valvano was – and continues to be – the very essence of that word!

JVH: When he announced the formation of The V Foundation, he created the motto that still resonates today: *Don't give up! Don't ever give up!*

After his announcement, money poured in from everywhere, from people who wanted to help play a part in creating The V Foundation. As we speak, donations of over $27 million have funded 170 research grants. The foundation operates with a small staff, a nationwide volunteer network, and an all-volunteer Board of Directors and Scientific Review Committee.

My dad's spirit continues to drive the work and growth of The V Foundation. These folks, along with ESPN, who has adopted The V Foundation as their charity, all give 110 percent, and are committed to keeping the original purpose, mission and focus alive.

It still amazes me that one man, with a notepad, a pencil and a dream, could create such an active, powerful foundation. And most impressive of all is the fact that 85 cents of every dollar raised is available to fund cancer research. Oops, I sound like a commercial, don't I?

LPG: You have a right to! The V Foundation is something to be very proud of. It is a phenomenal accomplishment.

JVH: I just wish I could capture the essence of Jim Valvano in words, but he was bigger than words … bigger than life! He lived with a passion for life, and he never let circumstances define him. That is such a powerful legacy. He made me realize that one person really can make a difference. With all the turmoil in the world today, I believe his message, his philosophy, his passion is more powerful and more relevant than ever!

LPG: What would you say is the one piece of advice Jim Valvano would give to someone who is struggling with adversity, and is in need of rekindling?

JVH: He would reach out and hug you, smile that great big grin, look you right in the eyes and say, "It's always too soon to quit! Don't give up. Don't ever give up!"

On April 28, 1993, just a month after his unforgettable speech at the ESPY's, Jim Valvano died of cancer. He was only 47 years old, yet he had accomplished everything on his list. His spirit is as alive as ever, and his legacy continues to inspire and influence people around the world.

To learn more about The V Foundation, and to make a contribution, visit their website: www.jimmyv.org.

 Jamie Valvano Howard is the "middle" of the three Valvano daughters, and is a 1995 graduate of North Carolina State University. During her father's illness, she suspended her education to spend time with her family. She has enjoyed success as a middle school teacher, an event planner at The V Foundation, and as a motivational speaker. She is married to her high school sweetheart, Matt Howard. They have two sons, Jake and Grant, and live in Cary, North Carolina.

If They Could See Me Now

- Mark Drury -

Just one time in your life, do something that every-one says you will never be able to do.

I really love that piece of advice. I first heard it back in early 2000, but it wasn't until the summer of 2002 I decided to take that advice and "push the envelope." I was sure from the start that I had bitten off more than I could chew.

I had lost an unbelievable 150 pounds when June 2002 rolled around. I was eating clean and exercising like never before. Just three months earlier, I had taken my pressed nose off the window of the YMCA group fitness aerobics room and wandered in to take my first class. It was the beginning of a love affair.

That first class I took was called *Body Pump*. It is a high energy, muscular-endurance, barbell aerobics class, consisting of 10 tracks of pulsing rock, dance, and club music choreographed to work 10 different muscle groups to exhaustion. It sounds tough and it is tough – but I just loved it, loved it, loved it. When the class ended on Monday night, I just could not wait for 48 hours to pass so I could take it again on Wednesday night. Three weeks later I was basi-cally living for *Body Pump* classes.

I was feeling better than ever with my weight loss. I was also escaping the clutches of diabetes, congestive heart failure, sleep apnea, and clinical depression. I was on an "upward" spiral. My good friend, Rosie Dunlap, from the YMCA, showed me a pamphlet from AFAA, the Aerobics and Fitness Association of America. They are the governing body that certifies health and fitness instructors. Rosie suggested I might want to challenge myself by applying for certification as an instructor. She told me I could do it. I read the pamphlet, then put it in the back of my mind. Who was she kidding anyway? I used to weigh almost 400 pounds and had been morbidly obese since high school. Two short years ago, I could not even tie my own shoes. I never ran more than one block since I was nine years old. To top it all off, I had recently had heart bypass surgery.

About a week later I was taking *Body Pump* class and we were lying on our steps, bench pressing to Guns 'n Roses wailing away on "Sweet Child O' Mine." I hate that song. Then the idea struck me. I wanted to be on that platform teaching that class! If I were king, I could select the music I liked and teach the class the way it should be taught. I wanted to be the guy everyone else was looking up to for leadership, encouragement, and motivation. Where in the heck did I put that AFAA pamphlet anyway?

I called AFAA and ordered my textbooks. It cost about $150 just for the books alone. The last time I cracked a textbook was for my advanced taxation final in college in May of 1978. Trying to read something and commit it to memory at age 47 was very tough. This was basic anatomy, physiology, exercise theory, and fitness theory. I dragged that *Fitness: Theory and Practice* textbook everywhere I went for four months: doctor visits, office lunch breaks, ball games, restaurants, church – you name it. If I left the house, that book was under my arm. We were as one.

The whole time this mental osmosis was underway, I also had to get my physical act together. I began getting coached on everything I might be called on to do as part of my exam. I was being hoisted in the air trying to master a chin-up. I was crunching my abdominals. I hired a choreographer. I was hovering, doing pushups, stepping, jumping, running in place, running for distance – and all the while thinking to myself, "Who in the world are you trying to kid?" Then I remembered that advice, and I answered myself: "I am doing something that everyone says that I will never be able to do!"

I persevered. I did a little bit more. I amazed myself! The first time I did 10 pushups on my toes, I felt absolutely unstoppable.

On November 16, 2002, at 9:00 in the morning, I signed up to take my certification exam. It would be over at 7:00 that evening, and cost me about $400. As I got out of my car and walked toward the gym, I could not believe I was actually doing it. I was still quite overweight. In fact, I weighed in at 222 pounds the day I took that test. It was just one year after my heart attack and heart surgery.

There were four other men and three women taking the exam along with me that day. They were all very lean and fit. I was a "work in progress." I remember lying on the wooden aerobics floor doing pushups with some man kneeling down beside me, watching my form and checking my breathing technique. I kept thinking, "I am doing this as an inspiration to every one of those 16,000,000 morbidly obese people in the United States who think that there is no hope for them. I am going to do this if it kills me."

I jumped a little, stretched a little, ran in place, ran a mile, kicked, curled, and got up and down off the floor at least 100 times. The hardest part was leading a class for the first time, being critiqued on my style, vocal cueing, projection, class flow, and technique. The day ended with a written exam of 150 multiple choice questions. Believe me, I was whipped when I walked out of there that day. Then began the long wait for the letter in the mailbox.

The promise of results in four weeks became the reality of results in seven weeks and four days (but who was counting?). Then it arrived! I opened the large envelope with one big rip, and read the words:

*"We are sorry to inform you, but you did not meet the
requirements for certification."*

I had passed every part of the physical exam and failed
the written exam! The greatest irony of my whole life. My
whole life I had been a brilliant scholar but unable to catch
a Nerf basketball. Now I am 47-years-old, able to do
pushups on my toes and run a mile, and I fail the lousy written test. I was so incredibly upset.

After a few days, I called AFAA and rescheduled the
exam. My good friend, *Fitness: Theory and Practice*, and I
became inseparable. On January 26, 2003, I took the exam
again, and I was ready! The entire week before, I would look
at a stranger, point and mutter to myself, "Clavicle, ster-
num, humerus, radius, ulna, rib cage, biceps, triceps,
deltoids, lats, abs." I knew my material. And when this
exam was over, I knew I had done well.

On February 14th, 2003, a walk to the mailbox brought
tears of joy to my eyes. The results read:

"Congratulations on your new achievement."

I had done it! I was now certified in group exercise
instruction – theoretical and practical … which means not
only do I know what I am talking about, but I can actually
get up there and perform it as well. There is a newly-framed
certificate hanging on my media room wall that brings a
smile to my face every time I look at it.

I was out of my comfort zone. I was aware of the fear,
but I went through with it anyway. Facing fear makes the
next experience even less formidable.

People are much less likely now to tell me that I will
never be able to do something. It is a wonderful feeling. So
I encourage you: *Just one time in your life, do something
that everyone says you will never be able to do.* You may
just surprise yourself!

The Subconscious Power of Music:

Listen Up or Tune It Out!

- Theresa Behenna -

*W*hen you hear the song "New York, New York" being played, how does it make you feel? Do you find yourself kicking up your heels? What happens when you hear Elton John's "Candle in the Wind?" Do you think of the tragic loss of legendary Marilyn Monroe and Princess Diana? Whether we realize it or not, music can put us in a mood that affects our behavior for better or worse. For me, it nearly cost me my job.

As a professional pianist from Australia, I used to travel around the world playing the piano in wonderful five star hotels when I landed a contract in Germany. The Munich Hilton Hotel attracted a lot of executives from surrounding offices to its elegant piano bar after work. It was an authentic piano bar with a grand piano and stools around it.

My knowledge of the German language consisted of one word: "Ya" – meaning "yes." (For a single young lady traveling on her own this was not always the best choice of words!) One evening a man came up to me and asked if I knew how to play a particular German song. I didn't. Somehow in half German and broken English he managed to ask that if he bought the music for me to read, would I be able to play it then? Being so new to Germany and eager to please, I said: "Ya!" and thought no more about it. A couple of nights later the bar was crowded with a lot of business people and I had every stool occupied around me at the piano. Up came the man with a sheet of music in his hand.

The title of the song and the lyrics were all in German so I had no clue as to what it was. I began to play the music.

All at once there was a deathly hush throughout the entire room. The people sitting close to me around the piano were looking at me very strangely. It seemed the whole bar had stopped operating completely. The atmosphere had turned dark and tense.

Suddenly the General Manager of the hotel came dashing up to me with a security guard by his side. He grabbed the sheet of music from the piano and passionately tore it up into little pieces in front of everybody. Then he turned to me and shouted: "Don't EVER play that music in this country!"

I was stunned, frightened and confused. How could a single simple song cause such a shocking reaction? What had happened to the uplifting energy that was present just a few minutes ago? Then I found out. The song I was playing had been written under Hitler's rule. The words were all about Nazi Germany being the supreme ruler of the world. It was a song of racial superiority in the worst sense. No wonder every one had stopped dead in their tracks! This song reminded them of a horrifying time in their past history. Shameful memories of war and human injustice that they would just as soon forget if they could.

Music holds the power of joy or pain, focus or distraction, serenity or agitation.

What are YOU listening to?

Tune into a good mood the next time you're sitting in traffic on your way to being late for work, dreading that morning staff meeting. Turn on your favorite radio station. Pop on the CD that always soothes and inspires you. Listen to the tape that never fails to make you sing along.

Feel yourself uplifted and ready to face the day's challenges. It's quite magical.

It's all in the power of music.

Easy Listening Can Change Your Life

- Jeff Davidson, MBA, CMC -

*E*asy listening music can have a dramatic effect on your well-being. Some people enjoy listening to soft rock or classical music while they work, and others do so for leisure. Whether you appreciate the slow pace, enjoy the absence of distracting words, or simply like benign background noise, you can use this music to handle the challenges that may come your way, and improve your lifestyle as a result.

Music can help in the treatment of pain management, depression, anxiety, even helping those in the grieving process or those facing terminal illness. Music can even produce physiological benefits, not just psychological ones. In his book *The Art of Preserving Health, Book 4*, author John Armstrong in the 1760s told his reader, "Music exalts each joy, allays each grief, expels diseases, softens every pain, subdues the rage of poisons and the plague."

Music in Surgery

Today, as a result of extensive research on the dramatic impact of music on one's psyche, we know that music can calm patients headed into surgery, reduce post surgery healing time and need for medications, and potentially lead to shorter stays in the hospital overall. Dr. Bernie Siegel in his book *Love, Medicine and Miracles* observed that even patients who are heavily sedated can "hear" what's going on in the operating room. So, positive, uplifting statements by the medical team, as well as relaxing music, do have an impact.

Music for Improvement

Listening to classical music, and to Mozart in particular, can promote learning, healing, and personal calm. Researcher Don Campbell calls this the Mozart Effect, and says that it can help to organize the firing patterns of neurons, which can stimulate creative thinking, strengthen your focus, and calm your nervous system. In a manner of speaking, your subconscious is "always listening." Hence, music can have a significant impact on your soul and psyche as you prime yourself to move into some new space on the road to rekindling your spirit.

Mother Nature's Music

Another form of easy listening that doesn't involve music is that of the soothing sounds of nature. A variety of vendors including Sharper Image, Radio Shack, and Best Buy offer soothing sound-systems, usually no bigger than a radio or cassette player. These systems enable you to select the sound that you find most appealing. For example, you have your choice of ocean waves, gentle rain, wind whistling through the trees, or birds in the forest. You can program these systems easily to play all night, or to be the gentle sound that greets you in the morning, or to play for a defined period of time.

Most systems come with headphones for private listening as well as powerful speakers that could sound-condition an entire room or more. Another sound device is a white noise machine. It emits different frequencies and amplitudes of a droning, non-disruptive blanket of sound.

Relaxation Tapes

Your typical bookstores, health food stores, and some gift and specialty shops offer relaxation cassettes designed specifically to assist you with resting your mind and body.

Some tapes help you to focus on your breathing, which in itself can be a powerful and deep form of relaxation.

Some tapes offer affirmations. These are statements that, when repeated over and over again, can sink into the depths of your psyche and actually help you to move in your chosen direction.

Subliminal tapes are another form of cassette tapes that help you relax or achieve some other particular goal. There has been much discussion and debate over the years as to whether or not subliminal tapes are truly effective, and if indeed you even need them in order to make progress towards your goals.

Subliminal afficionados contend that our subconscious mind can interpret and process information at far greater speeds than our conscious mind. The subconscious mind, proponents claim, does not need to weigh the data or attempt to put things in order. When it hears a message repeated often enough, it acts on that message. The intro-duction of subliminal tapes has significant efficacy.

Those opposed to the subliminal tape process argue that this is precisely the reason why it is best not to use sub-liminal tapes. Who wants a message directed to your subconscious over and over again, even if it is positive? Why not allow both your conscious and subconscious mind to work for you in unison to help you make progress?

If you are curious about exploring the world of subliminal tapes, whether it is for relaxation, goal achievement, weight con-trol, accumulating wealth, or many other re-invention focus areas, simply get on the Internet and type in the words "subliminal tapes" on any popular search engine, and you will get dozens of hits.

Allowing yourself to completely relax by listening to something soothing can be a great addition to your daily life. Take time out for easy listening, and renew your mind and body in the process.

Pass It On:
The Gift that Keeps on Giving
- Edie Raether, M.S., CSP -

*A*s I reflected on what the perfect piece of inspiration would be to share in this anthology, my mind floated back to a woman I had met during a program I presented many years ago. I remembered she had an amazing story that truly personified the idea of *rekindling*. That memory triggered a frantic search to locate her, so I could recapture her experience. Believe it or not, I was able to track her down, and with her permission, I share her unbelievable story with you now:

The "Happy Days" were for more than Richie Cunningham. Janice Williams Valentine can testify to that! When Janice graduated from Attucks High School in Indianapolis, Indiana, in 1957, she aspired to set the world on fire. Her parents had just gone through a bitter divorce, but Janice had won three Oratorical contests – providing the funds to attend Indiana University in Bloomington, Indiana. However, money soon ran out and she could no longer stay on campus. With empty pockets, she returned home and finished her freshman year at the university's extension in Indianapolis, where she began her service to humanity at LaRue D. Carter Psychiatric Hospital. At age 19, her exceptional character and intelligence were recognized by a psychiatrist who urged her to contact Earl Wilson regarding financial aid or a scholarship. Although the physician was referring to his friend at the University of Indiana, Janice only knew of one Earl Wilson, the infamous syndicated columnist of the *New York Times*. Being a zealot for opportunity, Janice contacted the compassionate columnist to publish her plea for someone, anyone, to provide her with a loan for college so she could fulfill her dream of becoming a social worker and helping those in need. Her ending words – words that began a chain reaction of human help – were, "I'll pay it back – honest I will."

Although many readers, movie stars and plain people too, sent in money to pave her path, a generous woman from Pittsburgh committed to pay for Janice's entire education, with the understanding that Janice would never know her name.

Janice mirrored the gift of giving, and while in college took a job at a dentist's office to help her mother with expenses of six younger children. After graduating from Howard University in Washington DC, Janice immediately "passed it on" by returning part of her income to the Earl Wilson Fund, so others could benefit from the eternal gift. While there was never direct communications between Janice and her secret benevolent benefactress, Mr. Wilson, the columnist, was a conduit and kept the two informed.

The rewards of contributing to the growth and actualization of another's potential to make a difference apparently became intoxicating for the benefactress, who seemed to be suffering from withdrawal. To maintain her addiction to altruism, she now offered to fund a graduate degree for Janice, again providing living and miscellaneous spending money as well. At the graduation ceremony a couple of years later, Janice reported that she could feel her fairy godmother's presence and imagined that somewhere in the audience were two smiling eyes with gently rolling tears and two hands silently applauding. When we can see the invisible, we can do the impossible.

When Janice later married Don Valentine, she expressed a desire for the donor of her destiny to share in the celebration. But her silent benefactress remained true to her desire to remain anonymous, sending instead a very treasured gift which reflected the hands of fate and the hearts of faith.

Now, years later, Janice is in a position where she is able to help disadvantaged college students and struggling women trying to improve their circumstances. In these efforts she, too, remains anonymous.

As I once again experience the goose bumps from Janice's story, I am reminded of the power of an individual's influence on others. It started with the suggestion from her professor to make a contact. It continued with Janice's willingness to take action. And with her action came the ever-present synchronicity of Janice writing to the "wrong" person, which led to the right person who could help her the most.

We may never realize who we help, or who is helping us – but the important thing is to keep the cycle going. Through the continuous flow of positive action, the universe is able to connect people and resources in powerful ways that can rekindle the human spirit beyond your wildest imagination!

When your true purpose is to help others succeed, you succeed.

-Bud Coggins

First Solo
March 9, 1994
- Dan Thurmon -

*T*awoke to an overcast morning, then called the automated weather information line at the airport. Ceilings were 1,300 feet, which meant it was probably not a good day for flying. I called my instructor, Mark Milam, to confirm that my lesson was off, a bit relieved.

"No, come on in" he said, "we are just going to stay in the pattern today, so we won't need more than 1,000 feet. The weather's perfect." My heart skipped as I realized that there was no backing out. Today would probably be the day of my first solo – the culmination of commitments I had made to myself and my teacher.

Commitments are how we define our character, and they come in different degrees. I have always been fascinated by flight. As a child, flying was often the subject of dreams and fantasies. So, when I was formulating my "life list" of experiences and achievements I expected to achieve, "Learn to fly" was a natural. I wrote down the goal and committed to following through on it at some point later in life. While this was an important step, it was only the first level of commitment. I committed to the process and goal in my mind, and I wrote it down to make it real.

The next level of commitment is when you begin to take action. With my pursuit of my pilot's license, this came about five years after I made my list. My wife gave me her full support to go after my dream. We were newly married with no kids yet, so I sensed that if I didn't commit the time

31

and money now, it might be a long time before I could pursue this goal. So, I went to the local airport, met an instructor, bought my books and other materials, and had my first lesson.

As of this day, I had acquired just over nine hours of flight time in the pilot's seat. And during every flight, I had the assurance and presence of my instructor in the seat to my right. It was comforting to know that even if I made a mistake or forgot a procedure, he would be right there, just in case.

Take offs and landings are the most important and potentially dangerous portions of any flight. The key to a successful career as a pilot, it is said, is to have your take offs and landings come out even. This was the focus of our lesson today. That is why we stayed "in the pattern." This meant that we would take off, turn left four times, making the box that defined the flow of traffic before landing. We would climb to 1,000 feet, the clouds seemingly right on top of us, then descend to the runway, performing "touch-and-go's," following each landing with an immediate take off. I was doing all the flying. After repeating the procedure eight times, Mark instructed me to land the airplane, then taxi back toward the runway and stop the plane.

Once I complied, my instructor did something that made me extremely uncomfortable. He got out of the plane. "Now just do the same thing again, Dan. Then come back and pick me up, OK?" This was the moment I had been anticipating, but I didn't think it would come so quickly. Not today, after only nine hours of practice. Surely he didn't really think I was ready.

"Are you sure?" I asked.

"Sure, I'm sure. I've never lost a student yet. Don't screw up my record."

That was reassuring, in a way. He thought I was ready. And so did I. I pushed the throttle, moving the plane toward the runway. I radioed the tower, requesting permission to take off. "Gwinnett tower, Cessna 67318 in position, runway 7, ready for immediate departure."

"67318 you are clear for take off. Runway 7." That cinched it. Even the guy in the tower thought I was ready to solo. So I moved the plane onto the runway and followed the routine we had practiced, all the while talking to myself. You see, wearing a microphone and headset, when you speak you can hear your own voice amplified. The words are only broadcast when you push the button. To me, this version of an amplified pep talk was useful. I can't recall everything I said, but it was very stream of consciousness.

"OK, Dan, you are going to fly a plane today. You know how to do this. Let's get going now. Push the throttle. Oh yeah, that sounds good. Hold the centerline. Watch your airspeed. Oil pressure Ok. Relax ... Yeah, right. Speed's increasing. Approaching 60 knots. Begin to rotate. Pull back ... And ... we're off the ground!"

When the wheels left the runway, my first thought, honestly, was "Why did I do that? There's no way out of this now." Then the realization came. Now, I must follow through with this goal. There is no turning back. This is the moment I realized the third level of commitment: when there is no turning back. Because of your actions, you must continue forward. You have passed the point of no return. At this level, your senses are peaked and you find the resources you need to make it happen – because you must! So, I kept talking, except the talking unconsciously became more like singing.

"I'm flying a plane. Flying a plane. How about that? I'm flying a plane. Climbing to 500 feet. Time to turn. Here we go. Make the call." Then I composed myself and in my best pilot's voice, broadcast to the tower. "Gwinnett tower – 67318 turning left–crosswind runway 7. Gwinnett."

Climbing and singing, I reached pattern altitude, just below the clouds. Another call. "Gwinnett tower, 67318 turning left downwind runway 7. Gwinnett." The airport was laid out perfectly just outside my window. It looked right. I had gauged my turn to be the appropriate distance from the runway. Not too close. Not too far. I kept an eye out for traffic as my plane became parallel to the spot I hoped to land. Just two more turns. A little more singing.

"Carb heat out. Throttle back to 1,700 rpm's. Looking good. Now some flaps. Ten degrees. Here we go." The increased flaps and reduction of speed started my descent, and after a few eternal seconds it was time to turn again.

"Gwinnett tower. 67318 turning left base, runway 7."

"Add more flaps. Twenty degrees now. We are coming down, down, down. Keep the airspeed up." Out my window, I could see the runway getting lined up, and it was time for my last turn.

"Gwinnett tower. 67318 turning final, runway 7." And I did. Watching the runway lights that serve as a guide, I could judge that my approach path was slightly high. Add flaps. Thirty degrees. And let that nose come down. The lights turned from both white to white and red, indicating I had fixed my angle of descent. The next moments seemed like slow motion, as I glided down toward the ground. Watch your speed. Keep it down the middle. Get ready to level out above the runway right about … now.

The plane remained above the ground for a few more seconds, then lost the speed and the will to fly, easing down to the runway with that wonderful "squeak" of rubber on asphalt. I did it. I had followed through to myself, my instructor and my goal. What a relief. What a moment. I taxied the plane around to Mark, who was watching with a big smile on his face. I approached with confidence and opened his door to take him back to the flight school and complete the lesson.

"That was great," he said. "Few people ever have the experience of soloing an airplane. And, today, you did. Now do it again. Then come back and pick me up." He closed the door. My lesson was not over.

I did three more take offs and landings. They came out even. Each time I expected the lesson to be over, and Mark would ask for "just one more, than come back and pick me up." They became easier and more fun. The singing continued, but the voice steadied a bit with each time. My confidence grew.

I am grateful for the way my teacher pushed me when he knew I was ready. He also knew how to keep me focused on just the next moment. There's a great saying among pilots: "When in doubt, fly the plane." With all the activity that makes up flying – communications, navigation, looking for traffic, monitoring instruments – at times it can be overwhelming. But the saying goes, "When in doubt, fly the plane." In other words, regardless of what else is happening, the most important task is to make sure the plane stays in the sky. Fly the plane.

Through this experience, I learned a lot about commitments. They come in stages. The first commitment is when you commit with your mind. Next, it's when you commit with your actions. And, finally, there is no turning back.

So take a look at your goals, and ask yourself how committed you are to accomplishing them. I encourage you to take that big step that catapults you into step 3. And if you're worried about all the details, just remember: "When in doubt, fly the plane!" *Happy landings!*

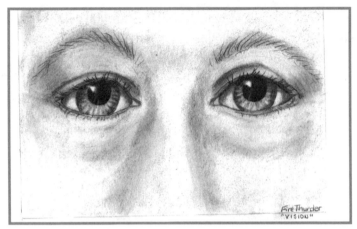

(Artwork by Colleen Fire Thunder)

These Eyes

- Sarah Starr -

These eyes have seen a lot of life through tears:
Some tears of joy – some tears of bitter pain;
Days followed days and mellowed into years,
And life was ever changing – and the same.

These eyes drift back to days that long have past.
Regrets, though small, are often in their sight.
A "might have been" a cloudy shadow casts
And anxious thoughts desire to make it right.

Then to the future visions bright unfurl,
Great dreams and hopes await their turn to be,
And big "what ifs" around the eyelids curl
And opening, worry what these eyes might see!

Back to the present do these eyes return,
To live but day to day – the past to earn.

Brown Eyes

- Janis Nark, Lt. Col. USAR (ret.) -

One of the most difficult things I had to do in Vietnam was to send someone back into battle. These young men had seen the face of war, heard the deafening noise, tasted the fear, had their buddies blown away, and been wounded. Wounded – but not bad enough to get their ticket home – and now had to go back to the field.

They always seemed to know when it was coming. As well as I felt I knew my patients, I could never know for sure just how they would respond. Some would just sit there and nod their heads as their eyes lost focus to some distant place in time. Some would cry and beg us not to send them back. Some went AWOL.

He was in his 20's. I have a picture of him, still. He looks like he could be 40. He wasn't the average 1970 GI. He was a soldier, and he took his job seriously. There was something very strong and quietly powerful about him. He moved with the grace and stealth of a panther, all of his senses keen, alert, ready, waiting, every muscle in control.

Unlike the "mother" role I took with most of my patients, I felt very much like a woman with him. He unearthed in me all the feelings that very early in my tour I had learned to suppress. I felt very small and aware of myself. We would talk for hours, sometimes about the war, but also about so many other things. I felt like he knew everything. When he looked at me I felt naked, and he was always looking at me. Sometimes I could make him laugh and his brown eyes would dance. But most times when I looked into his eyes, it seemed they were bottomless with pain.

I don't know when the war ended for him. I won't look to see if his name is etched in the black granite of our Wall. I want to believe he lived to earn lots of stripes on his sleeves and lots of ribbons and medals to wear with quiet dignity on his chest. I want to believe he's retired now, fishing somewhere, proud of his service to his country. I want to believe that he is physically healthy and mentally at peace.

I do believe that, even if I hadn't sent him back, he would have gone anyway.

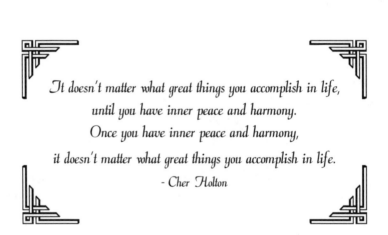

*It doesn't matter what great things you accomplish in life,
until you have inner peace and harmony.
Once you have inner peace and harmony,
it doesn't matter what great things you accomplish in life.*
- Cher Holton

Matthew, The Magic Crystal, and the Stanley Cup Playoffs

- Marty Clarke -

On April 16th of 2002, I was able to give my 7-year-old son, Matthew, an answer to the question he had been asking me daily for nearly two solid months.

Matthew: "Dad?"

Dad: "What's up?"

Matthew: "Dad, if um, if the season ended today, would the Hurricanes make the playoffs?"

I was pleased to tell him that finally the regular season had ended and indeed our beloved Hurricanes had made it into the playoffs. In the first round our boys would be facing the hated and feared New Jersey Devils who, only last year, had knocked us out of the first round in six games.

Matthew: "You think we'll win?"

Dad: "Well, now, the Devils are tough. They handled us pretty good last year and if they get the goaltending they're gonna be … "

Matthew: "I think we'll stomp them."

Dad: "Hmm … "

Matthew: "I think we'll score one hundred goals."

Dad: "Excellent attitude. Keep it up for tomorrow night."

Matthew: "What's tomorrow night?"

Dad: "Tomorrow night is Game One. Canes versus Devils and you and I will be there. Look at these."

I handed Matthew a pair of Stanley Cup Playoff tickets, Round One.

As an aside, if you ever have the opportunity to electrify your 7-year-old son, well, I hope you do it. Feels great.

When Matthew returned from the moon, he became his usual, practical self.

Matthew: "Are you going to wear your jersey?"

Dad: "Of course I am."

Matthew: "Me too. I'm going to wear my jersey too. But I'll take it off when we get ice cream."

Dad: "Good plan."

Matthew: "'Cause if they have the green kind I'll get the green kind but if they only have the vanilla Oreo kind, that kind still has dark in it and it could get on me."

Dad: "I think we're going to be fine, jersey wise."

Matthew: "Dad?"

Dad: "What?"

Matthew: "I think I only want the vanilla Oreo kind. I don't want the green kind, but if they only have the green kind. I'll get that."

Dad: "Let's put those tickets on the fridge."

Fast forward to the next night. Game night. At about 6:45 p.m. Matty and I are in our jerseys with a pair of tickets to Game One of the Devils versus the Canes. Oh yeah, playoff hockey. Matt is amped. Not only are we going to see a playoff game, but this is also a school night. This is what we call a "special exception."

The cool thing about the playoffs is you arrive at the rink in the daylight. For 97percent of the regular season you arrive in darkness. But the playoffs are different. I think it has to do with the orbit of the Earth around the sun or daylight savings or something.

Anyway, we have no parking pass so we have to park in the gravel pit near N.C. State's Carter Finley Stadium. Because Matthew asked me at every stop light during the ride to the arena if we were going to make the opening face off or not, I'm trying to hustle him inside. But as soon as he gets out of the car he starts picking up rocks and checking them for possible value.

Dad: "Matt. Matt. Matty! C'mon now, we need to ..."

Matthew (holding up a rock): "Dad this is Quartz. Quartz is inside rocks."

Dad: "Matt, put the rock down."

Matthew (not even looking at me yet): "It's not even quartz! It's a crystal!"

Dad: "Matt, we do not bring rocks to a hockey game."

Matthew: "It's a crystal."

Dad (dusting Matt off): "Fine. But we are going in now. Put the rock down and if you still want it when we get out you can pick it back up and bring it home."

And so off we went.

Inside the house was as loud as I had ever heard it. The Hurricanes hung tight and beat the Devils 2–1. Excellent. I love a playoff win.

Matty and I emerged from the arena concourse into the warm Carolina night along with about 18,000 other people. Spirits were running high. Hootin' and hollerin' all around. Halfway to the car the following conversation ensues:

Matt: "Dad!"

Dad: "What's up, my man?"

Matt: "Dad, guess what's in my pocket?"

Dad: "I know it's not that rock from the parking lot."

Matt (stops walking, and with a giant smile on his face, holds up a white rock): "The Magic Crystal."

Well, it is what it is.

Dad: "The Magic Crystal indeed."

Matt: "You wanna hold it? You can hold it if you want."

Dad: "No way. I'm not touching that thing. Only you can touch it. It's a seven game series, brother. Let me suggest this: you and I are probably not going to get to another playoff game. We're going to have to listen to the games on the radio in your room like we always do."

Matt: "Chuck Kaiten with the call!"

Dad: "That's exactly correct. So I suggest you place the Magic Crystal on top of your radio, and that way it will ..."

Matt: "It will send powers into the radio and out into, into ..."

Dad: "Into the network."

Matt: "Into the network! And then into the ground and then the Hurricanes will receive power!!"

Dad: "My point exactly. I mean it may have used up its powers tonight, but we better not chance it."

Matt: "Right."

Matthew was asleep in the back seat well before we got out of the parking lot and onto Blue Ridge Road.

But if you went into Matt's room that night, or any night during the 2002 Stanley Cup Playoffs, you may not have noticed it, but if you looked closely, you'd see the Magic Crystal sitting directly on top of his radio.

Everything we have is because
we knew we would have it.
Everything we are, is because
we knew we would be.
Our thoughts are our reality, good or bad.
We create our existence every moment
by what we think, what we say and what we do.
You are more powerful than you know.
Visualize often, well and especially specifically!
Live by choice, by intention, not by chance.
Above all, enjoy the journey.
- Janis Nark, Lt. Col. USAR (ret.)

The Gift of Giving

- Gail Ostrishko -

It is more blessed to give than to receive.
–Acts 20:35

*W*e all grew up with this timeless scripture, but knowing and living this principle requires life experience with both giving and receiving, and the paradox of reciprocity in both. I was an adult before I fully embraced this powerful universal principle of life.

My paradigm shift came years ago at the beach, on a women's church retreat. We were discussing stress reduction and life balance strategies when my friend quickly identified her top choice: Doing something nice for someone else. I didn't get it at first. Being raised in a family of limited resources, I had never really connected the two. Of course, eager to try something new, I quickly discovered it really works! I was amazed at the joy I experienced as a result of giving and doing for others. Of course it depends on what you are doing and for whom, and even more important: how you give and why.

If you want to lift yourself up, lift up someone else.
–Booker T. Washington

Giving is a fine art. We often find ourselves in search of that perfect gift for someone special. It is a consistent challenge we all embrace in different ways. Gifts are symbolic gestures of our personal connection with and desire to please others. Their value is more intrinsic than tangible and our patterns of giving and receiving define our relationships.

44

This idea is revealed in a book titled *The Five Love Languages*, which identifies the most popular approaches to expressing love … through words, time, gifts, service, and touch. Each of us is unique in our approach, and tends to give in the way we like to receive.

When I was a child growing up, my mother asked for the same gift on every birthday, Mother's Day and holiday: Peace and Quiet. Of course we just rolled our eyes, seeking a more solid, tangible suggestion, something we could purchase and wrap for her to open.

Somehow, peace and quiet just didn't seem like much of a gift to me. Of course now I realize what a priceless treasure it was for her.

This experience reminded me of our tendency to give what we want others to have rather than being sensitive to what they actually want or need. It brings to mind the classic Golden Rule, which has since been modernized by the Platinum Rule: Do unto others as they wish to be done unto. This approach brings with it greater challenge as well as potential reward.

Give Thanks

Begin and end each day giving thanks for the many blessings in your life. Although some days this is easier than others, we can always find something to be thankful for. Giving thanks becomes a habit which shifts our focus from the lack in our lives to the abundance awaiting our awareness.

It is right to give our thanks and praise.

Giving thanks to others is also a gift, to both parties. The simple words 'Thank You' go a long way to express appreciation and value for others and their efforts. We all have a need to feel valued by and connected to others, and this is a simple yet powerful way to make that connection. I frequent Taco Bell and always enjoy the look of surprise when I thank the preparer of my food for a delicious meal.

Oprah Winfrey popularized this idea in several ways in years past. Keeping a gratitude journal is one tool for cultivating awareness of our blessings and making a habit of giving thanks. Written thanks are nice because they can be read and reread, and can remind us of times passed and blessings overlooked

We grew up being forced to write thank you notes for gifts and favors received. Remember those? What a fine lost art that is! I actually enjoy crafting words to capture the essence of my appreciation for others. I recently wrote notes of thanks to my friends for gifts from a shower. One friend quickly reminded me that it was totally unnecessary. At the same time another friend tore open her note and laughed with delight for my words of gratitude.

Give Encouragement

We tend to associate thanks and praise with one another, and praise taken to a deeper level is encouragement. The word *encouragement* comes from the French word *couer,* meaning 'heart.' It is the heart of instilling courage. When we praise and give thanks for others and their efforts, we build courage and self esteem which nourishes individuals and relationships.

Like thanks, encouragement comes in many forms, as well. Words, deeds, smiles, hugs, even experiences and rewards can be encouraging. Encouragement is a bit like salt … a small amount can make a big difference, and too much can be hazardous.

Encouragement is to people
what sunshine is to flowers.

Did you know that a smile is a universal language of encouragement? It is the only gesture that carries the same meaning internationally. A smile can melt a heart, it can rekindle a spirit. Smiling is healthy for everyone, both the giver and the receiver. It is difficult not to return a smile, and almost impossible to act mean while smiling

Give Your Time

Of all the resources we have, our time may be the most precious. It is both finite and non-replenishable, making it one of our most valuable resources. When we give of our time, we are placing value on the person or activity we are investing in. Our presence is often the most precious of presents.

When my mother was aging and becoming more dependent on her children, it was difficult for her to ask for help. A strong, independent single parent for many years, her pride kept her from verbally requesting assistance. Instead of asking for my time, she would often request a specific chore to be done at the time I was departing from our visit.

I finally realized that she was asking indirectly for my time and my presence. Though I would often stay, it was not until after her death that I embraced the full impact of the gift of our time together.

Now I give my time as a volunteer, delivering meals on wheels and granting wishes to children with life-threatening illnesses. I am careful to be patient, to listen, and to give of myself and my time in these relationships. Sharing the joy they experience as a result of my efforts is a priceless gift in itself, a classic example of the reciprocity of giving.

Life is a gift from God.
What we do with our life is our gift to God.

Some Guidelines for Giving

- *Give generously and genuinely:*

Give from your heart as God has given to you. Adopt an attitude of abundance, realizing that giving to others compounds what you have to enjoy. 'What goes around comes around' and in the Circle of Life, you've got to give more than you get.

"Random Acts of Kindness" is a concept popularized years ago to encourage this idea. The movie *Pay it Forward* demonstrates the domino effect that giving can have. I think everyone can see and appreciate the cost effectiveness of this philosophy.

- *Give Consistently:*

Whether it is old clothes and appliances to the thrift store, words of encouragement to a stranger, or a perfectly wrapped gift for a friend, give consistently to others. I enjoy traveling, and when I travel I often see items that remind me of specific people. I enjoy purchasing those items to send or share with my friends, reminding them that they are never far from my thoughts.

- *Give unconditionally without expectation:*

We learned this one the hard way recently, in our attempt to adopt a baby. After housing and providing for a pregnant teen with the agreement to enter an open adoption, she left town abruptly without notice. We were shocked and devastated, and had difficulty making sense of the situation. We had given so much, with great expectation of receiving a baby in return for our physical, emotional and financial investment.

Luckily I had recently experienced a paradigm shift as a result of a sermon at church. After years of desire and prayers for a precious child to love and to nurture, I realized how much we were giving in an effort to make that happen. The sermon shifted my focus from what we were about to receive to what we were giving to this mother, this child and to God by extending our hospitality and unconditional love.

This experience opened our eyes to the true meaning of giving without expectation and in some small way, helped prepare us for the heartache of the unexpected outcome.

Do not neglect to show hospitality to strangers, for by doing that some have entertained angels without knowing it.
–Hebrews 13:2

Giving is a fine art, cultivated by our desire to appreciate and connect with others and ourselves. Though we often give in tangible ways, it is the act of giving that is more precious than any gift itself. While I have emphasized the art of giving, do not underestimate the power and the gift of receiving as well. When we open our hearts to receive graciously and gracefully, we allow others to enjoy the gift of giving. This universal principle governs our experiences and rekindles the spirits of people the world over.

My Mother, My Friend
- Diana Hershberger -

I looked upon you as my hero
When I was but a child
To me you had all the answers
You were the reason for my smile.

Many years went by
And with time I grew
Seeking out my own way
No longer appreciating you.

We had our differences
Both you and I
Often bringing each other pain
Making each other cry.

Our relationship strained
So much good we left behind
Not knowing how to continue
Or share that which was in our minds.

Then one day I needed you
I didn't think that you would come
But you dropped all to be with me
Loss of words, totally struck dumb.

Could it be you'd always been there?
All I had to do was call?
Reach out my hand, just cry out
And find you loved me after all?

Then redemption began
Forgiveness brought warmth to my heart
Estrangement became hope again
We were given a brand new start.

Now I look upon you as my hero
Though I'm no longer a child
You are my mother, you're my best friend
YOU are the reason for my smile.

Stir Up the Gift

- Brian Detrick -

*A*s I write this on a cold February morning, it is easy for me to enjoy a warm house, and I think how often we take our modern conveniences for granted. If I need more heat, I simply turn up the thermostat. Years ago, I would have needed to build a fire.

When I was a small boy, coal furnaces were commonly used to heat buildings. One of my earliest childhood memories is a mental image of a man shoveling coal into the stove in our little rural church in western New York State. As the fire began blazing, a warm glow spread through the building on that bitter cold winter morning. I can also remember my grandfather shoveling coal into the furnace to warm his apartment building, near Pittsburgh. Even today, some of my friends and neighbors use wood stoves to heat their homes, so the art of building fires has not completely died out.

One way to get a good fire going in the morning was to add enough coal the night before so that the fire never went completely out. The fire was "banked" – covered with fresh fuel and some ashes, to ensure a continued low burning through the night. Then, the next morning, stirring up the coals and blowing some air into them would rekindle the fire. That was much easier than having to build a new fire from scratch.

The Apostle Paul used this fire-building illustration in his letter to a discouraged young pastor named Timothy. In II Timothy 1:6-7, he wrote, "Stir up the gift of God which is in you through the laying on of my hands. For God has not given us a spirit of fear, but of power and of love and of a sound mind." In the original language, the word translated "stir up" means literally "to rekindle," "to fan the flames" of a fire.

Timothy had reason to be discouraged. Piecing together the Bible references, we know that young Timothy was timid by nature, and his health was delicate. Paul had sent him on some difficult missions, to deal with serious problems at the churches in Corinth and Ephesus. Making his task more difficult, some of the domineering church members did not take Timothy seriously, because of his youth, and probably also because of his lack of assertiveness. Furthermore, Timothy's friend and mentor Paul was nearing the end of his life. Paul was writing to Timothy from a prison in Rome, and he knew that he would soon be put to death for his faith. In his letter, Paul offered words of encouragement to Timothy, exhorted him to be steadfast in his faith, and told him to fan into flame the gift that God had already put within him. Paul sensed that in the face of adversity, Timothy's spiritual fire was burning low, and he urged him to rekindle it.

Paul's words are good advice to us, too. All of your life, God has been building a fire within you. He has laid the coals, through your family background, your circumstances, and your talents and abilities. When, as a Christian, you received Jesus Christ as your Savior, God lit the fire, with the flame of the Holy Spirit. Now, He wants you to keep the fire burning, to rekindle it, to fan the flames.

How do we do that?

Use Your Gifts

God has given each of us spiritual gifts, to be used in the building of His kingdom. But just as we must exercise our muscles to keep them strong, we need to use our gifts, or they will atrophy through neglect. Timothy's gift was proclaiming the Gospel. Paul exhorted Timothy, "Preach the word! ... Do the work of an evangelist, fulfill your ministry" (II Timothy 4:2-5). Whatever specific gifts we have, we should continually use them for the building of God's kingdom and His church.

If you don't know what your spiritual gift is, ask God to show you. Here is a hint: it is probably something that you already enjoy doing. God's gifts to us match the passions that He has placed within us. The fire in your heart will stir up the gift. Whatever you love to do and are good at, do it for the glory of God. Try it out, see what works, and see how others respond to it. Does what you love to do meet a need in your church, your family, or your community? If so, stir up the gift, put it to work, and fan it into flame.

Listen to God Speaking to You

Luke's Gospel tells us about two followers of Jesus who were even more discouraged than Timothy. After Jesus' crucifixion, their dream was shattered. They had given up, and were going back home to Emmaus. Then, on their journey, the Risen Christ began walking with them, and He told them that Christ's suffering and death had been foretold by the prophets, and were all part of God's plan. "And beginning at Moses and all the Prophets, He expounded to them in all the Scriptures the things concerning Himself" (Luke 24:27). I would love to have a cassette tape of that Bible study! Later, the two believers said to each other, "Did not our heart burn within us while He talked with us on the road, and while He opened the Scriptures to us?" (Luke 24:32). They spent time with Jesus that afternoon, and His words rekindled the fire in their despairing hearts.

God still speaks to us today. He speaks to us through His Word. He speaks to us through prayer. He speaks to us as we meditate on the Bible, and the Holy Spirit still opens the Scriptures to us. In the hurry and frustration of our daily lives, the fire can die down, and the embers sometimes become dim. Like the disciples on the road to Emmaus, we need to spend time with Jesus and listen to Him. His words will rekindle the fire, and our hearts will burn within us.

Stay With the Fellowship

If one coal is isolated from the others, its fire will die down and will soon be extinguished. In the same way, if a Christian isolates himself from the fellowship of believers, the fire of the Christian life will become dim. The Bible tells us not to forsake the assembling of ourselves together, but to exhort one another (Hebrews 10:25).

God never intended for the Christian life to be lived in isolation. This is hard for an American society of "rugged individualists" to accept. I went through a period in my own life when I thought I could live a good Christian life by myself, and that I didn't need the church. As I learned the hard way, that doesn't work. God put us together in the church, to live out our Christian faith as a corporate body. In difficult times, when the flame of your faith flickers, you need the fire of your brothers and sisters in Christ nearby, to keep your fire going. Conversely, there are also times when others falter, and the strong flame of your faith can rekindle their spirits. Although some of us in our pride hate to admit it, we do need each other.

Use your gift, listen to God, stay close to the fellowship – and don't be afraid. As Paul went on to tell Timothy, "God has not given us a spirit of fear, but of power and of love and of a sound mind." Stir up the gift that is in you, and keep the fire burning!

I Will Walk Again

- Faye Fulton -

*T*his event happened 38 years ago. There isn't a day I don't think about this struggle and revel in the fact that I am still here. I believe my life was spared for a purpose, and this ordeal has always been my strength. When I face hard times, I think about this experience and realize if I could overcome the diagnosis I received in the hospital, I can survive and thrive in any circumstance.

In 1965, I was a fearless 9-year-old tomboy living in one of Europe's capital cities. Three years prior, my father's job had brought my family and me to the colorful and exciting island of Sicily. I quickly developed a love of all types of sports – roller skating, bicycling, swimming, playing soccer, etc. Since I spent most of my time outside, I became the neighborhood's token "American" girl. I had all sorts of Italian friends, but I also had American friends.

The soccer tournaments were always in April. On the first day of tournament play in 1965, I was eager to warm up the team. As the Captain of my soccer team, it was my responsibility to see that all players were accounted for and spent at least 10 minutes warming up. I wanted to win the tournament that year and I knew I had a good enough team to do just that. Twenty minutes before the first game, I became anxious because my star soccer player, Jim, had not arrived. I did not want to lose, and I knew without Jim we had little chance of winning. I decided to go to Jim's house and bring him back to the soccer field.

With Jim in tow, the two of us set out for the soccer tournament. We met up with two more of my American friends who were on my soccer team, Sandy and her brother Billy. As I stepped off the curb to cross the street, I shouted

55

something to indicate how little time we had left to make it back before the first soccer game began. In my rush, I had not done something my mother told me to do a million times – look both ways. Before anyone could blink, an Alfa Romeo going 60 kilometers per hour hit my right side and I flew up into the air. (Weeks later my dear friend Contessa Pignatelli, who had been standing on her third floor balcony, told me I had flown up eye-level with her.) When my body hit the pavement, my left leg was broken in 11 places and my pelvic bone was broken in six places.

The Alfa Romeo driver picked me up, placed me in the back seat of his car, and left the scene of the accident. Before he drove off, he told my friends he would take me to the hospital. My three American friends (the oldest one was 11-years-old) were horrified and, no doubt, in shock. The only thing left of me was one of my sneakers. My friends picked up the sneaker, then went to find my mother. My mother opened the door to our high-rise apartment and almost had a heart attack, because there were three children in front of her telling her the only thing left of her daughter was one red sneaker.

My mother did not like living in a foreign country and never took the time to acquire a good command of Italian. She always relied on me to be her interpreter. At that moment, Italian would have served her well. She was so rattled she could not drive and Pietro (the porter of our building) had to drive her to the hospital. Pietro was also the person who called my father, at his place of employment, to inform him I had been injured and, in fact, no one knew exactly where I was. My father and Pietro decided to drive to the nearest hospital. It was a good decision.

The driver of the Alfa Romeo turned out to be a member of the Mafia, as were the other two men in the car. I woke up in the back seat of that car in excruciating pain, frightened to death. Who were these cigar-smoking men dressed in dark suits, and where were they taking me? At first I thought they were kidnapping me, but we quickly pulled up in front of a hospital and they took me inside. I remember being on the emergency room table in horrible pain; I could not think of any words in Italian. I kept screaming my telephone number to the nurses in English. The Sicily of 1965 was a very different place than the Sicily of today. Very few Italians spoke English and most of the Italians did not like Americans. Finally, I remembered the numbers in Italian. But, of course, no one was home to take the call.

It wasn't very long before my mother arrived. She was hysterical and the condition her middle child was in did not help. When my father appeared, he became infuriated. He was angry because the medical personnel had not touched me. They refused to touch an American unless they had a cash deposit, and they wanted a substantial one. Because my father was the top person at his place of employment, he had access to the company vault. That night he borrowed a large sum of money from his employer, replacing it the very next day after the banks opened. It was a small miracle, because there was no other way he could have gotten his hands on that kind of money on a Wednesday night in Palermo, Sicily. When my father returned to the hospital and gave the money to the staff, then and only then were my injuries appraised and attended to.

I was placed in what my family and I jokingly called "Dry Dock." My father worked in the shipping industry and the metal contraption erected around my left leg, which resembled scaffolding, reminded him of one of his tankers in dry dock. The purpose of this contraption was to add weights to pull my leg and corresponding bones back into their proper place so they would align with my pelvic bones. It was a long, tedious process.

A few days after my arrival at the hospital, my father announced the doctors had something to tell me. Three doctors walked into my room and told me I would never walk again. It was the only time I have ever seen my father cry. But, I was a tomboy. The thought of never walking, running, skipping, or swimming again was inconceivable. I looked right into the eyes of those doctors and I said, "That's a lie because I will walk again." They could not believe a nine-year-old girl was so adamant and brazen. My father could not believe my response, either.

I never doubted I would walk again. It took me two years, but I did it. Two years in a child's life is an eternity. Those were two years of metal contraptions, surgeries, procedures, casts, wheel chairs, and crutches. At one point I was transferred to a special "Leg Hospital" in Rome. That hospital was full of children with polio, but it also had the best doctors in Italy who specialized in treating leg injuries.

The ordeal of my accident and the long struggle to recuperate changed my family dynamics. Visiting hours were short, but because I was a child, my mother and father were allowed to spend the night with me in my hospital room. My mother spent the night during the week and my father spent weekend nights with me. At first I had plenty of visitors. My friends would come by and my father's employees would stop by for a visit. The adults seemed to gawk and they were visibly sad, because they believed I would never walk again. After a few months in the hospital, the visitors stopped coming. My family and I were left to deal with this on our own.

There were many skeptical moments and several setbacks, but my family bonded together as a unit with a definite purpose – I was going to walk again. It's been almost four decades since my accident, and I'm still walking!

We Need to Dance!

- Cher Holton -

It's a scary, troubled world out there – And hope is running low;
Fear is chilling people's souls. The economy is slow.
We need rejuvenation – Rekindling – a chance
To generate some energy – Some joy! We need to dance!

When spirits fall like tumbling stones, and bad times start to sting–
When things look darkest, that's the time to break into a swing!
When life throws curves to block the way,
    And business growth is slow–
We need to get an "attitude" and generate a Tango!

When depression finds a home in you and steals your last hurrah,
When sleep is all you want to do – It's time to cha-cha-cha!
When the news and television shout with slanted journalese
That's the time to grab a partner and do a Viennese!

When your money starts to dwindle down
    And the future seems unsure,
And your heart is feeling heavy – A rumba is the cure!

If hearing news brings thoughts of gloom, conspiracy and plots;
You'll lift your spirits if you do a couple of Foxtrots!
And when rekindling is a must – When you tire of life's assaults–
Release your tension, take deep breaths, and then enjoy a waltz!

It's a scary, troubled world out there, but we still have a voice–
Amidst the dark uncertainty, we still can make a choice.
When everyone talks gloom and doom, we have to take a stance–
We can choose to be rekindlers – and then, we need to dance!

The Great Illusions

- Dana C. Foster -

A karate teacher, concerned that his students weren't grasping the fact that the Martial Arts were more than just kicking and punching, set his students down to talk after meditation. As one of the students, I took a seat on the floor, eagerly waiting to hear and be enlightened by his profound logic. However, the words that came out of his mouth were nothing like I would normally have expected to hear.

In fact, I thought my ears were playing tricks on me. Our teacher made this statement: "Pain and pleasure are just illusions; they come and they go."

After he saw that his statement wasn't registering, he repeated it. Well, I didn't know about the rest of the class, but boy, I was confused. After two hours of training and fighting, I was feeling lots of pain – no ifs, ands, or illusions about it!

He then proceeded with an example. He said: "Imagine someone you had a deep, loving, personal relationship with just contacted you and broke off the relationship. One minute you felt the pleasure of hearing from them, the next you felt the pain from what they had to say. Over time you continue to feel this pain, until one day you see someone else go by. Your heart starts pumping and you get those butterflies all over again, once you meet and begin building a new relationship with them.

"As you went through all of this, you felt both great pain and pleasure. However, it was all just an illusion. The pain and pleasure came and went, as you focused and stopped focusing on them; therefore, they had to just be illusions in your mind, no matter how real they may have felt."

Soon we began to ask many questions to try and accept this lesson, but our conditioning was the same as most of the rest of the people in the world. No one likes to experience pain; instead, they look forward to experiencing pleasure.

Our teacher then related his message to the study of Martial Arts. He said: "Learning to kick and punch is just a side benefit of the art. They help you get to self-control, and self-mastery of the body, mind, and spirit."

From that day on, our class began to train and focus more on the mind and spirit to help bring balance to our progress. Even though the lesson on pain and pleasure is still somewhat hard to digest, I've learned over time his teaching is so true.

All episodes of pain and pleasure have come and gone when I decide to change my focus to something else. Now I am able to switch the illusions to better serve my personal interest. In a responsible life, there are many things I just don't like or enjoy doing. However, as a responsible person, I realize these things must be done.

For example, taking care of my personal health is something that only I can be primarily responsible for. But over the years, the pain of working out on a regular basis, in my mind, weighed more to me than what I started to weigh from the great pleasure I got from eating all the unhealthy things I could get hold of. Finally, I decided to switch the illusion and focus on the pleasure of becoming healthy again, and the pain of eating all that bad food and all the damage it was doing to my body. It all goes back to self-mastery.

The teacher's tremendous lesson has helped me move closer to this goal and overcome many emotional obstacles in life, by working on the issue from the inside first – then taking action toward what's on the outside.

America ...
Our Entrepreneurial Spirit

- Bud Coggins -

As a lad of five years, the first life-changing event I faced was December 7, 1941 when President Franklin Delano Roosevelt announced to the Nation on radio (no TV then) that the Japanese Empire had staged an unprovoked air attack on our naval base, Pearl Harbor, in the Hawaiian Islands. Many American military lives were lost and our entry into WWII was declared. Growing up in wartime, I learned very early in life what the "American Spirit" was all about. At my young age, it was difficult to understand why our young men and women had to die in a distant land. I eventually came to understand that they were sacrificing their lives so I could grow up safe and secure in a country that values freedom, independence and the opportunity to make choices.

Throughout our nation's history there have been threats to our freedom and peace-loving culture. Those who have posed threats have always underestimated the innate passion for our freedom to choose and our "pit bull" mentality when that freedom is jeopardized.

History will record that, as tragic and despicable as the events of September 11, 2001 were, the determination, will and resolve of the American people prevailed. We will always remember the heroes who inspired us to move on with a renewed sense of importance in our personal and professional lives. The accounts of unselfish heroism will require a separate book from the collection of history books.

The same characteristics that define our American spirit also define our entrepreneurial spirit. Having purpose, passion, vision and focus determines the success of entrepreneurs and creates great leaders. It is not coincidence that our country has been blessed with great leadership in times of grave danger and threats to our freedom.

Men such as Woodrow Wilson, Franklin Roosevelt, Harry Truman and most recently George W. Bush did not choose greatness but were destined to greatness by the circumstances of their presidency.

While the magnitude pales in comparison to terrorism, we entrepreneurs face daily challenges that test our will and resolve; yet, we overcome, learn and grow as we continue our "journey of success." The entrepreneurial spirit of our country continues to make us the greatest nation on earth, providing us the freedom to pursue our passion for independence and make a difference in the lives of others.

According to *Webster's Dictionary*, the definition of entrepreneur is "a person who organizes and manages any enterprise, especially a business, usually with considerable initiative and risk." Christopher Columbus set the foundation for entrepreneurism, at great risk, by pursuing his vision of a different world. Much later, the Pilgrims risked their lives to create a society free to worship and free of oppression.

Often times, we forget the so-called "giants" of industry also began as entrepreneurial ventures fueled by a vision to create a better world. Our history books portray the likes of Thomas Edison, Henry Ford, Andrew Carnegie, the Vanderbilt's, and many others.

Like many times before, the future is uncertain; however, what is certain is that the entrepreneurial spirit that exists in America will prevail. As Americans and entrepreneurs, we have many new challenges to face. When we open our heart, eyes, ears, mind and renew our passion and determination that got us here … we will continue to live, work and thrive in "the land of the free and home of the brave."

Grandmother's TV Tray

- Bil Holton, Ph.D. -

*The following story is adapted from a well-known tale from
the Brothers Grimm, and has a powerful message for us today.
As you read the story, I invite you to look into your soul and see
if there is an inner wisdom speaking to you. Then ask yourself
what behavior you need to change, in order to rekindle yourself,
and those who are closest to you,*

Once there was a feeble old woman whose husband
died and left her with a place she couldn't take
care of, so she moved in with her son, his wife and their six-
year-old daughter, Jennie. The old woman's sight was
affected by cataracts and her hearing was poor. Her hands
trembled so badly that when she drank her hot tea, she
spilled more than she drank. Soup would fall off her spoon
and she would miss her mouth occasionally, dropping food
on her blouse is well as on the floor.

Her eating habits annoyed her son and daughter-in-law,
and her hearing difficulty caused them to have to repeat
themselves much too often. When she knocked over a glass
of iced tea one afternoon, her son and his wife told each
other enough was enough.

They set a TV tray for her in the corner of the kitchen
and made the old woman eat her meals there. She sat all
alone with tear-filled eyes while the others ate their meals in
the spacious dining room. The only time they spoke to her
while they ate was to scold her for dropping a spoon or fork
or knocking over a glass of water or iced tea.

One evening after dinner, little Jennie busied herself constructing what looked like a miniature Lego coffee table.

"What are you building, sweetie?" her father asked.

"I'm building a dining room table for you and mom," she replied happily, "so you can eat by yourselves in the corner in my house when I get big."

Wordlessly, her mother joined her husband and both of them watched Jennie piece the table together. It wasn't long before they were wiping tears from their eyes.

"This is so embarrassing," the young man said to his wife.

"And sobering," she added.

He immediately rose, went over to the TV table in the corner of the kitchen and put it away. The next morning his mother found herself back at the dining room table with the others. From then on she ate her meals with the rest of the family. Her son and daughter-in-law never seemed to mind when she spilled an occasional drink or dropped a spoonful of food.

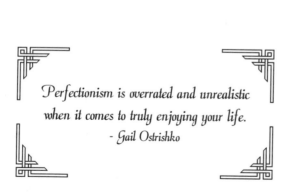

Perfectionism is overrated and unrealistic when it comes to truly enjoying your life.
- Gail Ostrishko

Permission to Let Go

- Ildeasela Buso -

One of the Muslim boys showed up at our back-
yard. He and another nine-year-old came to
recruit my son to join them in an urban adventure to the
park.

Soon my son and the boy whom I suspected was the
elected emissary, walked into my kitchen. I pressed my lips,
slightly twisting my mouth, greeting them with a stern look.

They ignored my attempt at intractability. Next time I
shall cross my arms across my chest.

They had a mission: permission for my son to go to the
park with them. He'd never been to the park without an
adult before. He knew he would need reinforcements to get
me to agree.

They were better prepared than they thought. The emissary had brown eyes.

Looking into these two beautiful pairs of big brown
eyes, one pair Jewish, the other Muslim, I succumbed to a
desire to see them smile.

"You have 30 minutes," I barked my permission, but
was unable to keep from smiling when their faces lit up and
they jumped to share the happy news with the scout waiting
outside.

It was a victory. For me. Uncertainty over overprotec-
tion. Let him play in the park, run with sticks, climb trees,
do whatever it is boys do at that age. That is why we live in
the city, rather than the suburbs, where there is no desig-
nated space for childhood adventures.

For the next half hour I couldn't cook or wash dishes. I
sat on a chair and methodically pushed away worrisome
images from my mind. The dangers of children playing too

close to the river. Injuries due to falling off of trees. Fights. Prejudice. Strangers feeling entitled to harass Muslims and their friends. Israelis and Palestinians unable to find peace.

When they came home, I was rewarded with the happiest two pairs of brown eyes I've ever seen. I knew I would embrace uncertainty again, next time. I was learning to let go.

(Artwork by Summer Fire Thunder, Age 9)

Relocation As A New Beginning

- Jeff Davidson, MBA, CMC -

At each point along your journey through life, whether it be because of mental or emotional pain or deprivation, a greater level of awareness, or consciously directed free will, you have the opportunity to renew yourself. To do so, it is important to examine how to leverage circumstances throughout your life. Various life passages, like the process of moving, hold rich potential in terms of renewing your life and rekindling your spirit.

You do not have to be the same person always living the same life, doing the same things. The opportunity to renew yourself – to make a notable change in your life, as in moving from point A to point B – is within your grasp. You can depart from what came before or embellish something already in place.

Seizing the Move

Most people move from their current residence following college, marriage, job opportunities, etc. With all of humankind's technological breakthroughs, one might expect that someone would do something about the onerous task of relocating. After all these years, there doesn't seem to be any way around loading and unloading every single thing you own, one item at a time, into a car or truck. You can hire people to do it, but the process of moving is probably no less upsetting. There are address cards to fill out, phone numbers to change, bills to reconcile, utility companies to call, and a ton of other activities to manage.

Determine ahead of time the specific changes that you want to make after your move. On a primary basis, you have to decide whether items will make the move, be sold, or be given away. This forces you to make decisions you wouldn't otherwise make when you're in the middle of a long-term lease and not considering relocating.

New Perspectives for New Times

More than the physical move itself, there's something about the moving process that is akin to changing. A move, like the start of a new year, is a place marker. It's an interval between one era and the next – namely, the time between when you lived in the former residence and when you moved to the new one.

In the new location, perhaps you not only want a new couch, but matching chairs and light fixtures to go with it. Perhaps your whole attitude changes. Maybe you decide it's time to upgrade your lifestyle and do more entertaining or associate with more movers and shakers.

You may be moving because you got a raise. In either case, the raise or the move, you have a new vantage point from which to view your life. From that vantage point springs opportunities for re-invention unlike anything you've experienced.

If you're married or living with a significant other, a move can be a wonderful time in which you mutually reinforce yourselves. Perhaps you agree to let your partner have more space in the new location, or you both agree to set up a home gym and buy some of those exercise machines advertised ad nauseam on television. Whether it's a move or any other element of your existence, exploit – in the positive sense of the word – the opportunity to renew yourself.

Before and After a Job Change

Relocation can occur without actually moving from one place to another. For example, looking for a job may be the start of an occupational relocation. Starting a new job, whether or not you are employed, creates a wide variety of challenges. In all of these cases, a great opportunity is presented for re-invention.

As emotionally nerve-wracking and financially destructive the job search can be, it is one of the clearest opportunities you'll have in life to contemplate the type of changes you want to make. After all, when else do you get uninterrupted stretches of time for determining exactly what's important in your life and career?

Still, it's easy enough to get caught up in the notion that "I've got to find a job, and find one now!" as your job search wears on. The feeling of desperation can haunt you if you're not careful. If you're currently unemployed, realize this is simply a transition period in your long-term career. Perhaps you got fired or left your previous job under less than pleasant circumstances. Maybe you're new in the workplace and have never had a career position. You may be re-entering the career world after many years. In any case, you're where you are for a reason, and you have before you the marvelous opportunity to set your sights on what is most appropriate, challenging, and enjoyable for you.

> *You do not have to be the same person always living the same life, doing the same things. The opportunity to renew yourself – to make a notable change in your life – is within your grasp.*

With Crystal Clarity

Try to recognize that establishing clear goals related to your next job may help you get a job more consistent and more aligned with what you want to do in life and where you want to be at this age. This way, re-invention becomes more than just a thought; it becomes a reality.

Some potential goal statements that may serve as starting points for your re-invention are: to land a full-time job by June 30th of this year with a salary of 10 percent more than your last position; to be employed in your industry as a manager at $38,500 or more within 120 days from now; to land a sales position with a top EDP manufacturer with a 10 percent commission rate, to begin at the end of this quarter.

Another goal may be to gain a summer internship with one of the Silicon Valley Internet service providers at an average of $15 per hour or more, two months prior to the start of the season. And, finally, to gain a year-long appointment to the special task force at my same salary, starting with the next fiscal year.

Milestones for the Taking

You may encounter career milestones that naturally prompt re-invention. These include a large pay increase, your appointment to a special/high office, your election as an officer in your professional association or group, an interview by a national publication, or the publication of your biographical information in a *Who's Who Directory.*

Some other non-career related milestones include an invitation to be on a special committee supporting your town council, a request from your local newspaper about your views on a community issue for their opinion page, or a decision by a literary magazine to publish your poem.

Whenever any of these kinds of events occur, given the new situation, you may find it fitting and appropriate to re-examine your life. Also, evaluate the other, more personal milestones in your life. For example, a four-year scholarship may mean that instead of your son or daughter working the summer before entering college, the whole family can go on an extended vacation.

Whether you are moving to a new location, a new place of employment, or a new stage in your life, the changes you are making provide new opportunities for re-invention. Take advantage of those opportunities, and renew your life.

The Secret to Success

- Dick Cheatham -

*T*he secret to success is simple. Let's get right to it. The secret to success is simply a person's realization that they have no peers. That's it. When you come to realize that you are unique, that you have a set of talents, skills, abilities, knowledge, interests and values that no other human has, then you have taken the very first and most important step toward success.

And as you are unique, so too are your "successes," for true success for any individual is inextricably linked to your personal values. No one can define success for you.

Those who do not know their values do not know themselves, and can obviously never succeed on their own terms. On the other hand, those who do know their own values but subordinate them to the values of others, are limited creatively. Any "success" they experience will be someone else's success and, at some level, they will know it.

There are legions of people out there who strut their "success" only to experience nagging doubts and regrets which they don't understand. In many cases, this is simply because they don't know themselves and their fundamental values well enough to know what is really important to do. They have been chasing successes which were not their successes.

By the time one has become an adult, if the process of self-evaluation has not become a regular on-going practice, one may be buried beneath so many layers of inherited "other people's values" that real success may never be possible. There is only confusion and disappointment.

Do not be fooled into thinking that making lots of money is success. Perhaps it is and perhaps it's not. Perhaps it's an indication of success, perhaps it has nothing to do with your success at all.

A practice you may want to consider in seeking that self-knowledge which is essential to success is putting your basic beliefs down on paper, and being as rigorous and introspective in the process as possible. Once one has completed that process, the results should be reviewed and the process repeated over and over at intervals for the rest of one's life, for we learn as we grow older, or at least we should.

Not only is this practice of value to one's self, it's also extremely useful to those who have connections with us. Providing a "Caveat Emptor" containing your most basic beliefs and values available to all who may be your customers or clients, your employers or employees, even your family and friends, can actually draw people to you who share your values. Not only might that assist you in your personal crusades, but it might save you and people who do not share your values a great deal of grief due to misunderstandings and unjustified assumptions.

You limit your success as soon as you define yourself within limits and definitions that have been designed and created by other people. Life is so rich, choices so plentiful! If there are any real limits to what humans can achieve, learn and experience about life, those limits are so far from us that we will never come anywhere even close to them.

One thing I recommend for anyone determined to know as much about life and about themselves as possible, and thus what success is for them, is to carry a pocket digital recorder for recording important thoughts and revelations. Writing is not always possible, so pencil and paper are not the best. Tape recorders use tapes which can too easily be replaced and stored indefinitely. These tiny digital recorders must be emptied periodically in order to continue to be of value. Thus one must deal with the recorded material, taking time to transcribe it and work on the saved ideas.

All great ideas, all achievements, all successes start with these very personal beginnings in our reflections, revelations and thoughts. On the other hand, following the crowd is not the way to start toward success.

Peer pressure can be very strong, especially for young people. Those who never grow out of that typical youthful focus and reliance upon peers can become adults for whom real success and happiness is always just out of reach. It's a sad fact that many adults come to settle into ruts that prevent them from ever plumbing the depths of their creativity, their passions, their joy. When societies become filled with such adults, those societies become static, often stratified with hard barriers between those who will not be limited and those who feel anger and envy toward those who will not conform. Liberty itself can become jeopardized when a large percentage of citizens in a society feel too comfortable and safe within the status quo.

My life's passion is ideas. I've always been fascinated by why people do what they do. This wonder, this curiosity is my first recollection as a young child. I still wonder why people do what they do. Some things people do I can easily understand. Some seem mighty weird! I came to realize early that different people saw "success" differently. And some of those "successes" didn't look much like successes to me. I was, as a result, drawn to a study of history, which is nothing more than a study of people succeeding and failing. And at least in free societies, each of us gets to decide which is which.

In investigating history, especially American History, I came to notice a certain common thread. Certain fundamental elements came up over and over in the successes of this special country. More than in most parts of the "old world," the American people seemed free and able to define their own values and actually experiment with and attempt to live by them.

My life's work involves discovering people and events in America's past which reflect what I've learned of life's fundamentals and then presenting those ideas in impersonations, or living history portrayals. Often people whose contributions to our lives are tremendous receive little if any credit. Described below are several individuals who, though typically attended by flaws as well as virtues, were able to find  their own successes. And their successes not only benefitted them, but have flowed through time to benefit us all today.

In the early 1600s John Rolfe, Pocahontas' real husband, fortunately knew he had no peers and followed his own values. As a result, literally years before the Pilgrims landed at Plymouth Rock, he saved the foothold of democracy which became America. He would not be lured into the pessimism held by most of his contemporaries who had come to believe there was no profit to be had in North America and were ready to give it up. He defined success for himself, finding it where others had missed it only because they did not recognize it right in front of their eyes.

In the late 1700s Richard Henry Lee, the man who made the declaration of independence which Congress voted upon on July 2, 1776, knew he had no peers and followed his values. As a result, he never let up in his lifelong quest for individual liberty. He came to realize his special facility with words, especially spoken words. Lee came to be known for the tremendous power of his orations for liberty, coming to rival even Patrick Henry, who was known as the "Voice of the Revolution." Lee, more than any other person of his generation in America, was at the center of events which brought independence to America, often as the primary catalyst.

In the first decade of the 1800s Meriwether Lewis fortunately knew he had no peers and attempted and succeeded in doing something that no one had ever done before, traveling thousands of miles across the North American continent and back. What others said could not be done, and many even said should not be attempted, he did. He defined success for himself, and fortunately so. His efforts helped to make this nation one which extends its special and unique system from sea to sea.

Just before the middle of the 1800s, President John Tyler realized he had no peers and thus almost singlehandedly prevented the passage and implementation of Henry Clay's "American System" which would have destroyed the Jeffersonian vision which Tyler held so dear. President Tyler was presented with challenges no president had been challenged with before. It would have been very easy for Tyler to define success as did most of his contemporaries in American government. Fortunately he did not and steadfastly pursued his most fundamental values.

These people were not different types of humans. They were much like you and me in most ways. What set them apart is that they knew they had no real peers. They defined "success" for themselves and then sought it. My friends, for our own sakes and for the people who care about us, we can and must do the same.

A Letter To My Granddaughters:

Jessica 15, Becca 15, and Summer 9

- Nancy Eubanks -

y Darling Granddaughters:

When my babies were placed in my arms for the very first times, I thought that I could never again be so filled with love for another human being – nor so completely depended upon. When each of you granddaughters was placed in my not-so-young-anymore arms, it was inconceivable to me that the same feelings came back to me. All the love and pride I had felt with my own babies washed over me again, and I realized how fortunate I was to have these wonderful bundles that I could watch grow and flourish. My responsibility to you was simply to love you and hopefully be loved by you. And I thank God in His Heaven that this love has far exceeded my hopes and I know, whether we are together or apart, that our love for each other is strong, secure and lasting.

I was asked what advice I would give to you grandchildren for the world in which you are going to spend your lives. I've given that a lot of thought and haven't come up with anything new, so whatever I say will be old news.

I think this world needs two things: 1) love for God, and 2) respect for our fellow men and

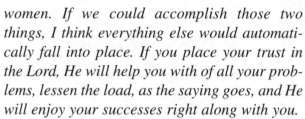

women. *If we could accomplish those two things, I think everything else would automatically fall into place. If you place your trust in the Lord, He will help you with of all your problems, lessen the load, as the saying goes, and He will enjoy your successes right along with you.*

If each of us respected friends, acquaintances and just the person-on-the-street, a newfound peace would eventually engulf the world. Oh, I know this will probably never happen all over the world, but it can completely encase you and your world. It has to begin with someone, and it might just as well be you. Just remember to make it contagious – spread it around.

There is something else we all need to do and that is open our hearts, ears, and feelings to God and to others. We must remember to stop and listen for His words and advice, and the words and advice of those who love us. Remember to hear with open minds and open hearts. That's important.

You know what I often say to each of you, "remember who loves you." You have my love and my prayers. And no matter where I am or whether I am around at all, my arms will always be wrapped around you, giving you warmth in the cold, strength in times of peril, and a full knowledge that I am rejoicing in your happiness.

Now, remember who loves you,
Grandmother

The Procrastinator's Mantra:
"I'm going to ... "

- Bud Coggins -

I'm going to start my new diet on Monday." "I'm going to stop smoking by midnight Sunday."

Do these declarations sound familiar to you? Have you said "I'm going to _____" (you fill in the blank)? Let he or she who has not uttered these words over and over again be the first to cast dispersions on those of us who are card-carrying procrastinators. The question is: Why do we have to be *hit upside the head* with a 2 x 4 before we actually take action and right a behavior we know is wrong for us? How can seemingly intelligent people continue to do stupid things that are harmful to their health? I'm not here to provide a "clinical" answer, but to ponder the reasons we knowingly continue damaging behavior.

Since Sir Walter Raleigh "discovered" North Carolina, it has been a birthright to smoke tobacco products. After all, they did name a cigarette after him. Even in the early 1960's, it was a secret that smoking could "possibly" be harmful to your health. As evidence began to come out of the closet, U.S. Congress banned cigarette advertising from broadcasting and required Public Service Announcements encouraging people to stop smoking. The culture of North Carolina began to change. In 1968, I was smoking four – yes four – packs of cigarettes per day. People would say, "How can you possibly smoke 80 cigarettes a day?" My response was, "I have to get up early and stay up late." At midnight August 18,1968, I pulled my last nasty drag of the "weed."

For me, going "cold turkey" was the only way. Five of my associates and I signed an agreement that whoever started back smoking would pay the others $25 each. Remember, this was 1968, when $25 got you a lot more than a few gallons of gas and a small latte at your favorite coffee shop.

This year (2003), only one other associate and I will celebrate our 35th Anniversary of not smoking. I am 100% convinced that I would not be here to tell this story today if I had not quit smoking. The irony is that as a totally positive person, I survived withdrawal by focusing on the *negative* aspects of smoking. Burned holes in clothing, stale smoke in car and office, and yellow fingers were compelling reasons enough to not smoke. But the real clincher was the constant plea of my two small children, who were asking, "Daddy, why do you smoke?" Try answering that question to a four- and two-year-old.

An offshoot to not smoking was a constant struggle to maintain weight control. All of a sudden, food really tasted good. So, a war against weight has been a long, hard fought battle. My three (one born in '69) children grew up hearing me declare, "I'm going to start my diet on Monday." I could not begin to count the number of Mondays that I "started my diet."

One of the great mysteries of life is that we know intellectually that a "diet" never works for most people. Emotionally, we are sure we can lose a quick 15 pounds and then return to those wonderful treats we sacrificed while "dieting." Hello, wake up and smell the hummus. It doesn't work that way. We each have to discover what inspires us to make changes that we know need to be made.

On August 30, 2002, I was really jolted by a heart attack that came with no warning. Over the years since 1968, I have constantly maintained at least a moderate exercise regimen an average of four days a week. Additionally, I have eaten fairly healthy food. Fortunately my cardiac event was a big warning. I got another chance that many people don't get with a heart attack. My cardiologist determined that with medication, increased exercise and a new approach to nutrition, I should live a normal life.

Talk about your 2 x 4 to the head – wow!

In the ensuing six months, I have been involved in a cardiac rehab exercise program at an outstanding medical facility specializing in heart disease. I've made permanent healthy lifestyle changes in my nutrition (by the way, hummus doesn't taste like "earth" as I once thought) and lost 20 pounds. My inspiration was, once again, thinking of the negative outcome (like a shortened life) of not making lifestyle changes. More importantly, a loving, caring wife and six beautiful grandchildren are inspiration enough to hang around for as many years as I have control over.

The good news is that healthy foods don't taste like the carton they came in, as they once did. Even though we are still a nation of extreme obesity, food manufacturers have found a market in those of us who have been whacked *upside the head* with the proverbial 2 x 4.

I'll leave you with this question to yourself: "What inspiration do I need to rekindle my heart, soul and body?" Once you make this discovery and take action, your self-worth will skyrocket. As Benjamin Disraeli stated over 150 years ago, "The secret of success is consistency of purpose." Have you discovered *your* life's purpose?

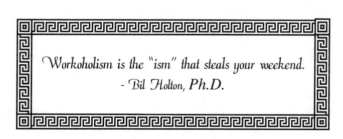

Workoholism is the "ism" that steals your weekend.
- Bil Holton, Ph.D.

Finding Life's Candles for Dark Moments

- Ana Tampanna -

*T*ragedy doesn't make an appointment. It attacks! A terrifying surprise that explodes in the midst of a family. Tragedy brings with it multiple consequences as well ... financial disaster, depression, guilt and blame. Devastating fallout! Marriages fall apart, family members commit suicide, personalities change. Yet tragedies occur daily. Tornadoes and earthquakes rip apart communities, car accidents claim thousands of lives, and children drink poisons or drown in swimming pools. People kill their friends and families, co-workers and peers. Here is what helped me make it through a horrendous time, so should it happen to you or to a close friend, you have some suggestions to fall back on.

Words Are Not Necessary - A Loving Presence Conveys Support

Initial shock and denial are numbing and intensely painful. When we received the dreadful news of our daughter-in-law's murder, we called our minister immediately. He and his wife came over and sat with us silently in the middle of the night. They made coffee, experienced our grief and comforted us with their presence.

Ask People You Trust to Handle Immediate Logistical Problems

We had to cancel plane reservations, and make new ones. Airlines offer a reduced fare for situations when grieving families need to rush in an emergency. My brother, who travels a lot, made reservations for us. Caring friends volunteered to keep our children and pets. Don't hesitate to ask or accept.

Keep Inspirational Reading With You

Ask your minister or a caring friend to loan you an inspirational book, if necessary. I found the book of Psalms particularly helpful, as well as a book loaned to me from an Al-Anon friend. Our minister mailed a wonderful book he had written. Another minister had comforting words about the sweet relief experienced when dying.

Keep a Journal

I purchased a thick, spiral notebook and kept it with me. In it I put information, as well as feelings, events, and questions. I taped business cards of police and investigators, and wrote down addresses of helpful strangers. My portable office became invaluable.

Buy Thank-You Notes

Thank-you notes help you to focus on the love and support you receive during this painful time, rather than your helplessness or loneliness. Strangers brought us food and took us to dinner. Our church sent flowers to our hotel room. Friends held mass at home for our daughter-in-law. People who admired her came to see us, gave us religious pictures, and bought us sodas. I concentrated on building a new support system by writing immediate thank-you notes. When we returned home, more thoughtfulness awaited us, including food, vitamins, and an invitation to go cherry picking (a perfect thing to do when processing grief).

Stay Connected To Home

If the tragedy takes you away from home, arrange a time when you will talk with a calm, clear-headed family member daily. My brother called me at four every afternoon. I looked forward to his call and found comfort in his familiar voice. I took my laptop computer with me, which enabled receiving caring messages via email. With my brother's phone calls and emails, our home community stayed informed of our trauma. They organized needed support as soon as we returned. The church "casserole brigade" had food ready, gift baskets, cards and prayers. A special service at our church and a prayer service with our Marriage Encounter Group provided us with loving friends who listened and cried with us as we worked through our emotional pain. One can't carry such a burden alone.

In the Months That Follow ...

Tragedies attract media, curious people, gossips, and people intrigued by dramatic life events. Sometimes people who had nothing to do with the tragedy become obsessed with the details. With our tragedy, information changed constantly, upsetting our perspectives and tearing our shreds of hope. Phone calls and emails came from strange sources. Be careful not to answer media questions or give out information to the wrong people.

A year might not be enough. Grieving takes time. Any healing does. For us, ongoing legal trials fester the guilt, doubt, and confusion. Even though life has basically returned to "normal," my energy level has not. I seem to accomplish far less than before. I remember having a long "to do" list and happily checking off task after task. Now, I check off two. (Three if I count my exercise.) My focus has become a wild animal, difficult to train. Yesterday, I had to write down 'take a shower.' Initially, I asked friends to take me places as a distraction. Immediately after I asked, it seemed as if I lacked time to go anywhere. Time became unmanageable. I let go of my career goals, a difficult challenge for an achiever like me. Making sales and booking presentations did not seem relevant any more. Even now, a year and a half later, I am still in the healing process, only now I have a deep understanding of what other people are going through.

Let go of what you didn't do to prevent the tragedy. Focus on what you can do to help others now. Both my husband and I have felt called to serve people in new ways. A year after the tragedy occurred, my husband was laid off his lucrative computer-consulting job. He wants to make a career change to teach high school. I took volunteer training to answer hotline phones for sexual abuse and family violence. The experience has been rewarding, and I'm sorry I waited until now to do it. Both of these activities stem from the helplessness we felt after our tragedy. We know our values are changing. It has been said that our tragedies make us who we are. We would agree with Corita Kent: *"Flowers grow out of dark moments."*

Sometimes our illness reduces us to our fighting weight.
- Bil Holton, Ph.D.

Words to Inspire ...
A Graduation Message
- Jeanne Sharbuno -

When I received an invitation to my cousin's high school graduation, it occurred to me that graduation isn't only about graduating from school. It can also be about graduating from a certain phase in life – or about graduating to a higher level of understanding in living life.

These graduations deserve our congratulations and acknowledgment, too. All of us are graduating in some way. I'd like to share with you the graduation message I wrote to my cousin. Perhaps you'll find meaning in it for yourself or for someone close to you.

Dear Wendy,

As you step out into the world, you may find that there will be people who want you to be just like them. Those who will want you to think, be, speak, and act as they do. That's about who they are, not about who you are. Stay true to yourself, Wendy. To what's most important to you, to what's right for you. Acting from your own integrity takes great courage. And you will be constantly challenged. Yet by coming from your truth and your heart's desire, you will have real happiness.

I'm reminded of a quote by Renee Locks, "The challenge is to be yourself in a world that is trying to make you like everyone else." Rise to this challenge, rather than let it get you down. Always remember, Wendy, that you are very unique with your own special inner brilliance. Let it shine through you day after day. It's a gift you give to yourself, your family, those close to you, and the community you'll serve. There are many of us behind you who love you and support you as you begin this new stage in life. Know that you are not alone. Know that you are blessed. Know that you are good enough. Know that the world is a much better place for you being in it.

My wish for you is that your 18th year, your graduation, your college years, and the years beyond will bring you a wondrous song in your heart and a lively dance in your step.

You're a very special young woman, Wendy. May all your dreams and more come true.

Love, Jeanne

My wish for you is the same. You're to be acknowledged and congratulated for your own graduation. As you move on to the next level in the school of life, let these words linger in your heart and help you to live successfully … from the inside out.

A Little Sunshine for Grandma
- Bil Holton, Ph.D. -

This story is adapted from a retelling of "Little Sunshine"
by Etta Austin Blaisdell and Mary Frances Blaisdell.

*O*nce upon a time there was a four-year-old girl named Mya. She loved her grandmother who was very old, wrinkled and white-haired. Her grandmother lived with Mya and her parents in a large house that sat on a hill.

Each day the sun peeped in the east windows, bathing everything inside with warmth and light.

Her grandmother's room was on the west side of the house, which was adjacent to a wooded lot. The sun never made it to her room.

One day Mya asked her father, "Why doesn't the sun want to peek into Grandma's room, too?"

"It tries to, but the trees are too tall," replied her father.

"Then let's cut the trees down."

"We can't do that, darling, the trees belong to our neighbor."

"Well, then, let's turn our house around."

Her mother overheard the conversation and came out of the kitchen.

"Our house is much too heavy," said her mother.

"And it would cost too much to have a contractor move it," added her amused father.

"Will Grandma ever have sunshine in her room?" asked Mya.

"Probably not, dearest, unless you can carry some to her," said her sympathetic mother.

Mya tried her best to think of a way to import sunshine to her grandmother's room. She asked the Sun to shine brighter. She prayed to God to help her. She asked the trees to grow a little slower and then recanted because she didn't want them to stunt their growth.

"I must take some sunshine to my Grandma," she said to herself. "My Grandma loved the sun when she was little like me. I'm sure she loves it just as much now."

When she was eating breakfast one morning, she noticed that the sun was shining in her cup of hot chocolate. She placed her little hand over the cup and rushed to her grandmother's room.

"Look, Grandma. Look! I have some sunshine for you."

When she took her hand off the top of the cut, there was hot chocolate in her cup, but not sunshine.

She frowned and left her grandmother's room. Later that morning she noticed a ray of sunlight shining on top of one of the books her father had written.

She ran over to the book and planted her hand on the cover, then raced into her grandmother's room.

"See, Grandma. Look. I've brought you some sun."

She lifted her hand, but the ray of sun had disappeared.

"Oh, I'm so sorry, Grandma. It was there a minute ago."

Her grandmother pulled her closer.

"The sun comes from your angelic face, my child," said her grandmother, "and it peeps out of your beautiful eyes. I don't need the outside sun when I have you."

Mya did not understand how the sun could peep out of her eyes or radiate from her face. But she was glad to make her dear grandmother happy.

From that day on, whenever she ran into her grandmother's room, she would blink her eyes to show their brightness and watch the smile which came back at her from her grandmother, who blinked back her own radiance.

Where are you spreading sunshine?

Ski Power

- Lois Gallo -

*C*ompletely bundled from head to toe with only my eyes and nose exposed to the frigid mountain air, I poised at the summit of the ski slope. My senses came alive as I drank in the glorious view of the resort and beyond. Suddenly I was overwhelmed with a sense of power, freedom, and well-being.

"Yes! I really can do this!" I was beginning to believe.

I looked down at the skis on my feet and glanced at my 11-year-old son zigzagging halfway down the slope ahead of me.

It was the third time I'd been down the beginner's slope since I had completed my first ski lesson that day at the Homestead resort in the western part of Virginia. I had come this far and had been successful in taking some risks and facing my fear of skiing from many years ago. Well, maybe it was really just the fear of risking the unknown … But anyway, I had faced my fear head-on and I was winning! It felt wonderful!

Go back with me just a couple of months earlier. It was October of 1992. My husband and I were both rising toward the peaks of our professional careers. We lived in our dream house and were involved in the community. This night we were preparing to go away for four days on a fall getaway to the Homestead resort.

All the arrangements had been made. The night before we were to leave, everything was packed. My mother had taken our son over to her place so we could get an early start on the drive to the mountains. This was a trip to a fabulous resort that we had eagerly been looking forward to!

At 2:30 a.m. my husband got out of bed complaining about the pain in his shoulders and arms. He thought his bursitis was acting up again, so he went off to the bathroom to take some strong pain reliever. I dozed back off to sleep, only to be startled from my repose by some strange noises in the next room. I called out to my husband as I stumbled sleepily down the hall to see what was happening. Through the door I saw my strong 49-year-old man slumped unconscious in the recliner. Quickly I called 9-1-1 for an ambulance. I just knew he must be having a heart attack and felt helpless to do anything for him.

Three days later, as he drew his last breath, I kissed my husband goodbye. But I was still in shock at the fact that I couldn't ask him anything again – and that all our dreams together were gone.

I vacillated between numbness and feeling so lost, interspersed with waves of sadness that would sweep over me without warning, triggered by a scent, a mannerism like one of his, a sudden remembrance of times we'd had or words we'd shared, seeing a loving couple together, or having a scenario pop into my mind that could no longer come true.

What was I going to do now? I had to start rebuilding and refocusing the direction of my life as a single mom. Already there were men I had thought of only as friends who now wanted to take me out to dinner, and who were viewing me in an entirely different way. I felt uncomfortable and wasn't sure how I should be relating to them. It all seemed so strange and difficult. Didn't they understand how much in love with my husband I had been? In my mind I was still married. No one's friendship could measure up to the years we'd been together and all that we had shared.

I finally realized I needed time to figure out who I was as a woman alone – without the identity of a man beside me – before I would be ready to relate to a man again in that way. Only then, I seemed to know, would I be ready to pick up the pieces of my life and move forward in a purposeful direction.

Until that time of healing and refocus would come, I tried to reach out to my son. I had to be mother and father to him now. We clung to each other to keep the memory of our past happy life together as strong as possible. But every day it seemed to slip further away. Although we cried together and then tried to accept it and go on, there was still a huge gaping hole in our lives. Our big house seemed so empty.

Finally I knew I had had enough. Things would never be the same, so something had to change in the way I looked at life. It particularly wasn't helping my son. So I did something bold. I made arrangements for the two of us to take the trip to the Homestead for Christmas, the one my husband and I had planned to take. We were going to initiate some new experiences and make some different memories for ourselves!

This Christmas was the first one without my husband and I knew it wouldn't be easy, so a change in place and venue was my way of not having to face a lonely Christmas at home with reminders of him at every turn. However, Christmas at the Homestead, as glorious and beautiful as the resort was, was probably even harder. We were surrounded by mostly families, with all their relatives coming in from everywhere to meet them for holiday reunions. And there were only the two of us – mother and son – knowing none of the other guests. That normally wouldn't have daunted me, as I easily make friends, but all the families were hanging out together and not looking to meet other people.

My son soon got over feeling that he had to hang out with mom – in fact, I encouraged him to join the other kids in some special resort-sponsored activities so he could have a great time. Now I was on my own to explore the resort. I decided to do something good for myself by experiencing the spa and its delights on the body. Then I went off on a photography walk to capture the wintry beauty on film. Soon I was acquainted with every area of the resort, but was still feeling lost and alone and very blue. Maybe this hadn't been such a good idea after all.

Well, there was one more thing we hadn't tried yet. With the gorgeous mountain range surrounding us, the resort had its own ski hills to master. They even offered lessons with Swiss ski instructors, plus a ski shop with rental equipment and all the warm clothes one would need.

Again I reminded myself that this whole trip was a new adventure: that my life had been given a twist, a turn, and that my vista had changed. I could never go where I had been heading just two short months before, and must now choose and be responsible for the choice I made for this day and the future days to come. All right! So why not finally face my fear and do something I would never ordinarily do – stretch myself and master a new skill? Why not be an example to my son – and empower him as well in the process of learning how to ski?

It was an amazing experience! We had a terrific instructor with a wonderful accent who made us feel we were getting ready to ski the Swiss Alps. And, best of all, he gave us the confidence, with one tiny technique after the other, that we could indeed gain control of that slippery slope and those two slender boards under our feet! And indeed we did! After an hour lesson and practicing a few moves together on our own, we were zigging and zagging down the bunny slope, being helped and even helping other struggling beginners up from spills along the way.

So here I was on top of a much bigger mountain in reality – and feeling powerful for having faced my fear and won! Would I go on to become an Olympic skiing champion? Probably not, and I may never even choose to go skiing again. But I celebrated mastery over the attitudes in my mind that had rendered me powerless in some physical sense. This physical empowerment then led me to a freedom in my soul and spirit. I released my fears and embraced the opportunities of the future.

I was finally free to walk forward on my new ski legs into the future, knowing even if I stumbled and fell, that there would be help around. And that I too could be a helper and a comfort to someone else who might slip and need a hand up on the slippery slope of life.

(Scott Friedman, CSP)

Our Extraordinary Interconnectedness

- Nancy Eubanks -

*S*ometimes it is amazing – and even eerie – how interconnected we are as human beings. It can manifest itself in amazing ways. Here is one example.

> *At age 13, my beautiful granddaughter, Jessica Scales, awoke from a deep sleep and realized that a poem was writing itself in her head. She grabbed a pen, and quickly wrote the poem entitled* My World.

> *When I read the poem a few years later, I dug through my memory box and pulled out a yellowed page, on which my daughter, Colleen (Jessica's mother), had written a poem when she was about 15 years old. I felt the goose bumps on my arms when I read the words I had written at the bottom of the page: Colleen woke up from a deep sleep and quickly wrote this poem. The title of Colleen's poem was* My Place.

My daughter and granddaughter share an amazing connection that transcends biology. The Muse of Creativity gently played through time and space to bring them to similar places at very different times.

With their permission, I invite you to read their poems and think about the synchronicity and interconnectiveness you've experienced in your life.

My Place

- Colleen Whitaker Fire Thunder -

On sleepless nights, I lie awake
And sort of drift away
To grassy turf beside the lake
Or a boat upon the bay.

Of all of these by far, I think
My favorite place to be
Is right there at the whole world's brink,
My place beside the sea.

Between my toes I feel the sand
While walking on the beach.
I take a star into my hand
And for the moon I reach.

The waves, they whisper in my ear
The songs of gulls in flight
As they roll against the pier
Beneath the pale moonlight.

Against my cheek, a gentle breeze
I smile, so real it seems
To be alone and so at ease
Beyond my wildest dreams.

Between my toes I feel the sand
While walking on the beach.
I take a star into my hand
And for the moon I reach.

So if I disappear, by chance
Then you'll know where I'll be
Where waves of water sing and dance,
My place by the sea.

My World

- Jessica Scales -

*D*on't be afraid to touch it.
It might bite you,
But it won't hurt for long.
Your garden of tulips might get flooded,
But it will dry in three days
    and a garden of roses will grow.

You might burn yourself on the stove.
It will leave a beautiful scar.
Your car might break down
    and after walking to and from work for three weeks,
You see things in the world you never saw before –
    amazing things.

Someone might die, someone close to you,
Someone you almost feel you cannot live without.
Your heart explodes, and while it bleeds,
    you discover pain.
You feel another emotion.
    … BEAUTIFUL …

You might lose a $50 bill, then realize
You would have worn those Tommy Jeans once
    and put them in your closet to mold.
So you decide to clean your closet out and give
    all those jeans to a woman you met
    when you were angrily walking to work
because your car broke down.
The lady lives in a box on the corner of Florida Street.
She got five new pairs of jeans today.
    … She loves the world …
    … It's a beautiful world …

Do You Live Your Life to Its Fullest?

- Marguerite Detrick -

Y *ou may be only two-thirds alive!*

That's a startling statement! Could it possibly be true of you? Certainly you want to live life to its fullest. The very fact that you are reading *Rekindling the Human Spirit* is evidence of that. But the suspicion that that statement might be true should be enough to arouse your curiosity.

Just what does it mean to be two-thirds alive? Simply put, you are a trinity, made up of Body, Mind and Spirit, and to deny any one of these is to deprive yourself of a full life. Each is important, and none should be neglected.

Of course, you recognize the importance of your body: farmers and manufacturers supply foods to nourish it; doctors labor to keep it healthy; diet gurus supply the means to keep it at the correct weight; physical trainers supply exercises to sculpt and mold it; millions of words are written to help you care for it; advertisers bombard you with methods of keeping it clean and attractive.

You know, too, how important your mind is: everywhere you turn you are reminded of that fact by a galaxy of media designed to entertain and educate – television, movies, radio, books, magazines, the internet; schools are available to impart every imaginable kind of knowledge; psychologists and psychiatrists use every means at their command to restore minds that are ill and to promote mental health in general.

Yes, without a doubt, you are aware of how important it is to have a strong body that houses a healthy mind. But what of that third part of you – your spirit? Could you be among the many who seem blind to the fact that they even have a spirit, much less realize the need to care for it? Or perhaps you are one of those who do recognize the existence of the spirit, but literally starve it by neglect. For, while they scrupulously feed their bodies three (or more) times a day, they expect their spirits to survive on a sparse diet, perhaps distributed once a week in a house of worship. Stop to consider what you are doing to yourself if you are denying your spirit its normal function. For it is a part of you – and it wants to live, fully and actively!

What, then, can you do if you suspect that your spirit might be the victim of your own neglect? Well, suppose you discovered that your body had been weakened by a deficient diet? Wouldn't you begin eating the necessary foods and taking the needed supplements to correct the situation? And if your doctor told you that improper breathing was keeping your body from functioning as it should, wouldn't you do the prescribed breathing exercises? Of course you would. And in the same manner, your spirit will respond to certain kinds of nourishment and exercises. If you are really interested in strengthening your spirit, here are a few ways you might do it.

1. *Practice Quietness.* One of the hardest things to find in this motion-mad world of ours is quietness. But its rewards make any effort worthwhile, for it is in an atmosphere of quietness that your spirit finds strength. Take time, in the midst of all your busyness, just simply to be quiet. And in the quietness, shut Self out, and let God come in. Shutting Self out requires real effort, so times of quietness are not necessarily periods of passive inactivity. They are times when you are actively responding to God as He says, "Be still, and know that I am God."[1]

2. *Talk With God.* Just as your spirit yearns for quietness, it also longs for communication with God. "Prayer" is the name that we have given to the experience of talking with God, and of it Tennyson wrote, "More things are wrought by prayer than this world dreams of."[2] But if we are to be honest with ourselves, we must admit that too often our prayers are not the kind that make things happen; they just don't connect us with God. We may feel like Shakespeare's Claudius, who, rising from his knees, confessed, ""My words fly up, my thoughts remain below: words without thoughts never to heaven go."[3] If you sometimes feel that you pray "words without thoughts," try to remember that prayer is not a monologue, in which you tell God what you want to have or do. Rather it is a conversation, in which you honestly try to find out what God has in mind for you, as you say, in effect, "Not my will, but thine be done."[4] And then, you really know what it means to talk with God.

3. *Read and Study.* Never before have so many books, tapes, and videos been available to stimulate spiritual growth. The Bible is published in many translations, written to make its words more comprehensible to the 21st-Century mind, and there are study books that will give a deeper insight to its teachings. New books are being published every day; spend some time in a religious bookstore, and you'll be amazed at the wealth of inspirational, educational and fictional materials being produced. And the internet is waiting for you to access its spiritual bounty 24 hours a day.[5] With such abundance, there is certainly no reason for your spirit to starve for want of "soul food!"

4. *Open Your Spiritual Eyes and Ears.* There are spiritual values to be discovered in the arts – music, painting, sculpture, photography, literature – with a wealth of inspiration just waiting for your interest. Here the public library can be of inestimable value in your research, not only for all the materials it has available, but also for any help that you might need in discovering available resources. I have found the people who work in libraries are eager to help, often going above and beyond what I ask of them – and always with a smile!

> *You are a trinity, made up of Body, Mind and Spirit, and to deny any one of these is to deprive yourself of a full life.*

The world around you also can open new vistas for your spirit. God's great, wide world becomes a more beautiful, wonderful place in which to live when you see it through your spiritual eyes. For me, even so simple a thing as the bird feeders that my son-in-law put up in my back yard give me delight every day. Watching the antics of the birds and squirrels, and knowing I'm in partnership with God in caring for them, give me a spiritual lift every day.

And every night, I go outside, or at least gaze through a window, to look up and marvel at God's handiwork. This is a habit born in childhood, when my mother would take me outside and name for me the stars and constellations. This was years before "light pollution" was dreamed of, and the stars shone brightly in an inky darkness; but even in this era, the heavens still declare the glory of God![6] Allow your spirit to enjoy all that He has given: mountains and sea, flowers and the trees, field and desert, birds on the wing and deer in the forest – all part of His creation, telling of His power and love. And all there to delight your spirit!

5. *Seek Spiritual Fellowship.* Your church offers you the fellowship that you will find so helpful in spiritual growth. But don't be content with once-a-week fellowship; most churches have seven-day-a-week programs, designed to meet the needs of every age and social group. If your church does not have a group for you, you might be just the person to stir up interest among others, and get one started. It is within the small group, as well as in the larger community of faith, that your spirit will thrive. The strength you will derive from the spiritual resources of others cannot be overestimated. And don't forget, your spirit has a sense of humor, as well as a sense of reverence, and it needs to laugh as well as pray. Good spiritual fellowship will offer the dimension of humor, too.

6. *Reach Out to Others.* Another exercise in which your spirit will thrive is in giving a part of yourself – your time, your talents, and your resources – to help someone else. Whether it be baby-sitting for the young couple down the block, giving a break to a harried caregiver whose loved one has Alzheimer's, painting the basement of the church, taking flowers to a nursing home, sewing for an orphanage, writing a letter or sending a card to someone who is lonely, making a phone call to a shut-in, saying a prayer to lift a burden – whatever you do for someone else will benefit your own spirit, too. Just look around you, and see how many things need to be done that could be done by you. Then get busy!

7. *The List Goes On . . .* Add your own examples of ways to strengthen your spirit.

The important thing is to discover those techniques that will be beneficial for you. Don't worry if you can't seem to get interested in one or the other of them, for spiritual tastes differ just as do physical and mental tastes. But with so many opportunities open, you need never again be satisfied with only two-thirds of a life. Whatever you do to enrich your spirit will not be wasted effort, but will continue to be a vital part of you no matter how many years go by. In fact, your spirit is the part of you that will live on when all else is gone, so every moment devoted to it now is really the best investment you can make for your future!

Footnotes
1. Psalm 46:10: The Bible.
2. Tennyson: Morte d'Arthur.
3. Shakespeare: Hamlet III.iii.
4. Luke 22:42: The Bible.
5. Three of many web sites giving inspirational materials:
www.upperroom.org
www.discoveryseries.org
www.americanbible.org
6. Psalm 19:1:The Bible.

A Successful Failure

- Alton Jamison -

$\mathcal{M}$y life has been filled with disappointments and failures. From growing up in a single parent home, where my mother raised me while my father was in jail, to being fired from my first job. Through my various trials, I have learned to endure the hardships and continue to strive for success. I have entitled this *A Successful Failure* for the simple reason that I was once a failure but now I am successful. I want you to know that regardless of your past mistakes, you still can become a success story. Over the course of my life, I have developed four principles that have guided me along the way. Please read these principles carefully and apply them to your life. Watch how you become a success!

⌒≡⌐

Crossover Principle

If you are familiar with basketball, then you will recognize the word *crossover*. Crossover is a common move in basketball (seen by the likes of Allen Iverson) where the player has the ball and fakes to go in one direction, then does a *crossover* with the ball and goes in the opposite direction. I applied this concept to my life and all of my failures. Early in my life, I appeared to be going in the direction that leads to dropping out of school and eventually going to prison. However, I choose to make a *mental crossover* and go in the opposite direction. Sometimes when you feel as though you are headed in the wrong path, you have to make a *crossover* and go in the right direction.

Ninth Inning Principle

In baseball, there are nine innings of play. If a team strikes out in the first eight innings, they still have another opportunity to hit the ball in the ninth inning. In this principle, you must realize that regardless of how many times you strike out, the game is not over until the ninth inning. Meaning, even though you may have made some mistakes in your life, the game is not over. You still have another chance at bat – an opportunity to try again. That's the awesome thing about making a mistake: when you try again, you will know what to do so you won't strike out the next time!

Resistance Principle

When you lift weights, especially bench press, the weights are pressing down on you. In order to keep the weights from crashing down on your chest, you must give the weights some resistance. Every time you push back with some resistance, you become stronger. Over time, as you continue to push back with resistance, that same weight will feel lighter and lighter. This is a very practical principle for facing adversity, including peer pressure, in your life. When people or things are pressing against you and you are in a position of making good or bad decisions, learn how to use this principle and begin to resist. Continual resistance builds your mental muscles. You will become stronger and eventually be able to overcome any adversity that may come your way.

The TKO Principle

In the sport of boxing, there is something called a *Technical Knock Out (TKO)*. Often times, this takes place when a boxer is knocked down three consecutive times in one round. How can this principle be applicable to your own life? You see, when statistics come your way, you must learn how to give them a TKO. For example, if a statistic says that you will not graduate or you will be just like your mother or father, then you have to keep fighting this statistic until you prove it wrong or *knock it out*. Sometimes, we focus too much on the limitations put on us by the statistics, instead of focusing on how to overcome them. Remember, when you are up against a statistic, take control of your own destiny and *knock it out*.

The Facts of Life

No matter how good the economy is now,
it will eventually take a downturn.
No matter how much your company loves you and you love them,
you may eventually have a falling out.
Your best customer may end up doing time
in the federal penitentiary.
Consumer reports may blast your product.
If any of those things happen, what will you do?????
Most people would say, "There's nothing I can do.
I'm a victim of circumstance!"
Bunk. No matter how bad things are,
the true winners keep on winning.
Maybe not quite as big or as much, but they still win.
That's because they're NOT victims of circumstance.
They're victors of circumstance.
When you can't control what happens, control how you respond.
- Mark Sanborn, CSP, CPAE

The Winning Ticket

- Debra Atkinson -

*E*ver buy a lottery ticket? Play Power Ball? Are you persistent? Bought more than one? Do it regularly? Just for the thrill of scratching off the card with the hope that this could be it?

Just what is "it?" Your dreams come true? Worry and care free? Everything you want, time to do it?

All the jackpots in the world can't buy health, can't guarantee a doctor can fix it if you've done too much damage or gotten an unlucky roll of the dice on that table.

What if you already held the winning ticket? There was no gamble – it was a sure thing?

Would you do it? Would you take those odds?

You might have to be more consistent. You might have to be more of a frequent flyer on this program, but it's a guarantee. Your odds are excellent that you reduce your risk for diseases that are a result of less-than-stellar lifestyle habits.

Play the numbers game with cholesterol, blood pressure, and your heart rate. You win.

No scratching involved, just blow the dust off your sneakers. You still think the lottery will afford you the 'good life' and provide all the things money can buy?

Your lottery winnings might buy the biggest house on the block, the fastest red convertible, the best seats in the house, but if your health doesn't afford you the opportunity to enjoy it, what's it worth? A reminder that if you don't take care of yourself early in life, it will come back to you?

Twenty-somethings, you may still occupy nearly-new bodies; they look good from the outside. You still have the benefit of high metabolism and you feel far removed from the threat of heart disease and cancer. You have "it won't happen to me" invincibility.

Thirty-somethings, you may be too busy chasing around your young family or giving birth to a career. Perhaps you're trying to enjoy your first real financial independence by doing things that keep you occupied without the additional burden of exercise on your schedule.

Forty-somethings, you may be feeling a little wear and tear on the parts, from all the labor with no regular tune-ups. The exterior is beginning to show a little use. You think a little more seriously about the need for health insurance by way of sweat-equity. But then again, your older family and involvement in organizations and clubs keep your time too filled.

Fifty-somethings, your aches and pains are talking louder to you, but you want to enjoy your empty-nest and still think leisure and social activities are a priority.

Sixty-somethings, your doctor finally says you need to address your health. You say 'no kidding.' You have the time, even the money to do what you want, but your body is less willing to cooperate.

Seventy-somethings, by now you wish you'd paid more attention to the 'sure-thing' that was right before your eyes so many years earlier.

The good news is that at any age, your odds of benefitting from a healthy lifestyle are a 'sure-thing.' Your chance of winning the lottery? Something like one in 125 million. Which odds do you like?

Heritage

- Ildeasela Buso -

"Mom, I am embarrassed to be part Hispanic."

"You are? Why?" I asked, amused.
"Because all Hispanics are crazy."
I laughed. "Really? How is that?"
"Well... I see it in you...and the rest of our family."

Hmm. I thought of my dad – a man who decided to shave his head and get an earring when it dawned on him that he was rapidly losing his hair and it was never coming back. "It's the only way I'll get respect now." The new look suited him, respect or not.

As for me, my son has been embarrassed far too many times when I can't stop from laughing at movies considered scary by the rest of the audience. And then there's the fact that I refuse to install a home air conditioning system. My philosophy: "To deal with the heat, act like a lizard: Don't move!"

So the family is a bit eccentric. Loco. Crazy. It's the family my son was born into, whether he likes it or not. But extending this individual observation to the entire Hispanic community was misguided. I scrambled to correct his generalization, while feeling defensive about my family's idiosyncrasies.

"Well, I'll have you know that there are plenty of Hispanic people living...uh...*normal* lives."

"There are?" He sounded hopeful.

"Lots! Many do not eat tofu or laugh during scary movies. There some who are even civil engineers!" I gasped, horrified, with a wink. "They constantly consult their oracle, the calculator."

We laughed. I hope his path between ethnicity and individuality is illuminated with laughter, humor and a capacity for wonder. *That would be heritage.*

Questions for a Funfilling, Joyous Year!

1. How many blessings can I be thankful for today?
2. Who can I positively surprise today?
3. What can I do to promote peace today?
4. Whom can I spread positive gossip about today?
5. What can I do today that will take me where I ultimately want to go?
6. Have I gone out of my way to make someone's day today?
7. Is there someone I can forgive today?
8. How can I maximize my uniqueness today?
9. What can I celebrate today?
10. Have I given myself an opportunity to laugh at myself today?

- Scott Friedman, CSP

The Visitor

- Lisa Church -

I've heard so many times that having a baby changes your life. But few things change your life the way losing a baby does. It's something I never expected to face, and yet so many women do. I became the one-in-three pregnancies that end in miscarriage. Not exactly what you expect when you're expecting.

I don't think anything could have prepared me for the weeks that followed my loss. The pain was so deep and personal that it passed through my body and struck my soul. I lost the life that was growing inside and I felt strangely numb. I was haunted by the child I would never see, or touch, or meet. There were no memories I could cling to, just an empty void.

Over time, the emptiness faded and slowly I began to heal. I knew I had to move on and I wanted to try again, but there was something looming over me. Fear moved into my life and it was settling in like an unwanted visitor.

So I waited and prayed and kept myself busy, but Fear did not move. Afraid to share this with anyone else, I confided in a friend who also had a miscarriage and was pregnant again.

"How did you get rid of the fear?" I asked her, ready to take any advice she could give me.

"I didn't," she said. "I'm still terrified everyday."

Her words hung in the air. I wasn't prepared for her answer. At that moment I realized that Fear wasn't going anywhere and my only choice was to face it. I decided to focus on my dream of having a family and try again. One month later my doctor confirmed that I was pregnant for the second time.

I shared the news with my family and a few close friends, who were ecstatic. I tried to smile and share in their joy, but inside I was terrified. When I got up the courage to tell my family how I was feeling, they reassured me that I would be fine in a few months. But as the months went on and the baby grew, Fear made himself comfortable. Every ultrasound was normal, every heartbeat exact – a perfectly healthy little girl was forming within me. Every thump and kick gave me hope that I would meet my baby, but Fear sat next to me whispering, "She might not come."

My family had moved on, and there was no way I could tell them that I was afraid to want my baby. I couldn't tell anyone. I put off decorating, buying baby clothes and even naming her, because I thought it would add to my devastation if something went wrong. This time I knew what was at stake and how much I really wanted this child.

Finally, the day I had waited and prayed for arrived. After 10 hours of labor, Fear was pushed aside and in my arms was my newborn baby. Everything I had been too afraid to want, but more afraid to lose, was tightly bundled and looking up at me. The joy and release and pure happiness of that moment will never leave my memory. Gazing at her tiny, pink face, it almost seemed fitting that she looked just like me. In an instant, I couldn't imagine my life without her.

Four months later, my baby girl greeted me one morning with a burst of spontaneous clapping and a gummy grin. Two years later, she stretched her toddler-sized arms around my neck and said, " I wuv you Mommie." It took everything I had inside to bring her into the world, but she's already given back so much; and there's more to come. To think I could have missed that!

I look at things differently now. Of course Fear still comes around, but now I know he will not win. And I realized if he stops visiting, I'm probably not attempting anything worthwhile.

Author Frederick Douglass said, "Without a struggle, there can be no progress." The struggle to recover from my loss taught me something. I found that courage is not being able to make fear go away – courage is moving on in spite of it. Conquering fear means living with it day by day, but never being defeated by it. My young daughter isn't afraid of anything, but one day she will have her own encounter with fear. When that time comes, I'll share with her the lessons I've learned and how she changed my life.

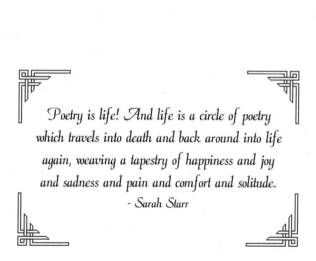

Poetry is life! And life is a circle of poetry which travels into death and back around into life again, weaving a tapestry of happiness and joy and sadness and pain and comfort and solitude.
- Sarah Starr

Blessings Of The Heart

- Shari Hudson -

*P*a-pum. Pa-pum. Pa-pum. As I lay my head on my husband's strong shoulder, I hear the beating of his heart: a slow, steady rhythm, a constancy that calms me. His soft, black tee-shirt caresses my cheek. The heat of his body comforts and soothes me. The slow rise and fall of his chest as he breathes reassures me. With a deep sigh of contentment, I whisper to myself that I am truly blessed.

I haven't always acknowledged the blessings in my life. Sixteen years ago my first husband filed for divorce and custody of our two small children. I won custody at the district court level, but my happiness was short-lived. The day the ruling was delivered, my ex-husband, upset with the decision, filed an appeal to the appellate court. The entire divorce and custody procedure took over two long years. The process was so painful that it didn't even occur to me to count my blessings. What blessings were there to count anyway?

Waiting for a decision from the appellate judges seemed interminable. I was anxious to know the outcome, but was also filled with dread. The fear of losing my children was immobilizing. We lived in a state of limbo, waiting to know our fate. Patience was definitely not my strong suit and I had never before experienced such a test of fire.

The appellate decision finally arrived and I found myself totally unprepared for the judge's ruling. Sadly, tragically, the outcome I had desired with all of my heart was not to be. With one fell swoop of the judges' pens, a two to one decision, my life was ripped apart at the seams. The ink, barely dry on the decree, glared viciously on the page. My hands and body shook violently as I read the judges' orders through eyes clouded by tears.

The decree required me to vacate my home immediately. I was ordered to reimburse my ex-husband for all of the alimony payments I had received. Physical custody was awarded to my ex-husband and I was given visitation rights. As I read the pages over and over, I could hear myself screaming "no" in disbelief. This just couldn't be happening. No matter how many times I read the words, the meaning never changed. I had lost my children. My two precious babies – gone. The pain was excruciating. Despair suffocated me. I didn't know what to do and was emotionally unable to do anything but sit and stare out the window.

The day after I learned of this horrific news, I received a phone call from a dear friend. Her brother was moving out-of-state and in a hurry to sell his duplex. Within three days of receiving the custody decision, I purchased his unit and moved into my new home. The duplex was small, and the children would have to share a bedroom. But it was just right for a single mom and two little ones who would visit.

Each moment I shared with my children, while limited, was precious and filled with joy. The majority of time, however, we spent apart. Seconds felt like hours, and days dragged on like weeks. Each moment I spent without them was agonizing and lonely. I couldn't bear to look into my children's empty bedroom. The open doorway was a bitter reminder that I was required to spend most of my time living without my beautiful children.

It took me several months to get over the initial shock of losing custody. My world, turned upside down in a heartbeat, forced me to make major life decisions. In order to earn a decent living and be a good example to my children, I decided to go back to college. I hadn't been in school for ten years, but if I was going to make something of myself, a college degree was necessary. I enrolled in a local university as a full-time student while also working a full-time job.

After two years of night school, I was awarded my Bachelor's Degree. I enjoyed getting my education, and four years later pursued and earned a Master's Degree in Organizational Management. Upon graduation I wasn't sure how my education could really benefit me. I just knew that getting my degrees were accomplishments no one could ever take away from me.

Over the next few years I worked at several companies, but still hadn't figured out what I wanted to be "when I grew up." Then one afternoon my life changed forever. The television in my office was broadcasting the Oprah Winfrey show. Her guest, Julie Morgenstern, a professional organizer, began speaking. I immediately stopped working to watch the program. I didn't realize it at the time, but God had intervened and set my life on a new course.

When the show was over, I somehow knew that professional organizing was the career for me. Within eight weeks I started *Organized by Design.*SM My new career as *The Master Organizer*SM and trainer were under way. Soon people began calling for appointments, and haven't stopped since. It has been a wonderful opportunity to help people, but this business has also turned into a blessing in disguise.

A year after I started my business, I married my wonderful husband, Roger. Neither of us had been to church in some time, and two months after our wedding we visited a church recommended by a friend. The sermon was on forgiveness, a topic that both of us needed to hear and something we needed to receive. The minister urged the members of the congregation to turn their lives over to Christ if they had not already done so. We could feel the power of the Holy Spirit at work and both Roger and I came to Christ and accepted Him as our personal Savior that very day.

It didn't take long for God to start revealing Himself to me. Although I didn't understand it before, I learned that Christ has a purpose for my existence. It involves more than helping people organize their desks or sort out their closets. My purpose is to serve my clients in ways that honor and help them work through their "clutter" in different ways. The blessing in disguise is the opportunity to serve others by sharing my story and to be a source of encouragement to those who feel that their lives are "out-of-order."

Later this year I'll turn 50, and as I look back over my life, I wish I would have begun a relationship with Christ years ago. Maybe then I would have known Christ began weaving Himself into the very fabric of my being long before my inception. I would have acknowledged Him and thanked the Lord for carrying me through the loss of my children, husband and house. I would have shouted praises to him for blessing me with a second chance at a successful marriage, family, friends, a new home, education, a promising career, and good health. At least now, I know better and am so thankful that God is at the center of my life. I am encouraged by His promise that He will never leave or forsake me, no matter what, and am assured that He will only give me what I can handle.

And so, here I am today, resting my head on Roger's shoulder, overwhelmed to tears by the very thought of God's goodness. The tears slide down my cheeks and dampen Roger's shirt. His heartbeat is strong and I am at peace, even though I think about what lies ahead. Within the year, Roger faces surgery to correct a defective valve in his heart. Of course we are not happy about his condition and are understandably concerned about the outcome. We pray for a successful surgery but we know there are no guarantees.

No matter what happens, during this surgery, or throughout our lifetimes here on earth, we have faith God has a plan for us and it is "just the right plan." As new Christians, Roger and I are excited about our walk with Christ and where His plan will take us. We know there is only one true "Master Organizer" and it isn't me. God has that honor. He has the title. He's doing the job. God is in charge, now and forever. Only He controls the slow, steady rhythm of life. Pa-pum. Pa-pum. Pa-pum.

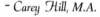

We can always learn from our mistakes.
Until we die, there is an opportunity to seek
or offer forgiveness, to improve relationships,
to reevaluate priorities and values and
to begin again.

- Carey Hill, M.A.

118

Put On A Hat And Fluff Your Hair:
Tricks To Look Better Than You Feel

- Jodie Vesey -

*P*ut on a hat, fluff your hair around your face, and you'll be just fine!" That was what my Grandma Kurth would tell her girls if they were having a bad day. Put on a hat to draw attention away from your less than smiling expression, and fluff your hair around your face to look perky. An instant disguise, of sorts, to get one through having to face others at a time when one would rather be alone. Although the hat part may be a bit passé, I think there may be something to what Grandma deemed essential to looking good. My grandma was a firm believer in lipstick and scarves, perfume and dress shoes.

I think of her as I am rushing out the door, already late, but needing to run back into the house to put on lipstick. I have discovered that the beauty of lipstick is not just skin deep – it is an instant pick me up for my mood, especially on my yucky days. There is saying that is quite simple: "Fake it till you make it." Herein lies the secret to looking better than you feel. The next time you are feeling blah about yourself, give one of these "fake it till you make it" tricks a spin. Who knows, you may end up seeing the sunshine before the day is over!

❖ Take a shower or bath and wash your hair. Imagine your bad mood going down the drain with the bubbles.

❖ Wear your favorite shirt and a pair of pants that are flattering. No fair hiding behind baggy clothes;

119

they speak loudly of your low confidence level, and you are sure to feel frumpy.

❖ Put on a pair of earrings or a bracelet – maybe something with a little jingle or sparkle to it.

❖ Wear a brightly colored top. Don't let your dark mood dictate your color choices.

❖ Add a scarf to your outfit. It looks light and breezy even when you are feeling low and blah.

❖ Buy a new shade of lipstick and put it on. An instant glamour pick-me-up!

And if all else fails, you can always put on a hat, fluff your hair around your face, and you'll be just fine.

The Weigh Out
- Mark Drury -

I began a seemingly impossible journey on October 1, 2000. I weighed 391 pounds at the time and I decided to lose 250 pounds. I eventually found out – one year later – why God put me in my car that particular Sunday afternoon and sent me to join the Northeast YMCA to get the ball rolling. The next 365 days would play out like an episode of *Touched By An Angel*. At about 50, I lost count of the angels God sent into my life that first year to make His plan happen.

I knew how to swim already and thought I would just swim laps three times a week. I was entitled to two free sessions with a personal trainer to get me up and running on the free weights and the Cybex weight machines. My trainer was George McCoy, the first angel on my case. George had lost 180 pounds in 1990 and has never regained one pound. He saw something in me that he knew he could keep going. I also bought a copy of Bill Phillips book, *Body For Life*, and began to eat clean and work out simultaneously for the first time ever in my life. I bought my first computer that month and went online looking for support – and found plenty of it. I learned about goal setting and about setting new goals each time I achieved a goal.

I was a house afire that first year. I had lost 30 pounds in my first month, 60 pounds in my first six months, and 90 pounds in my first year. People were noticing my weight loss, my clothes were falling off, and I was being reborn. Little did I know there was a monster under my bed. That monster was about to crawl out from under the bed and try to kill me.

Exactly one year to the day of my joining the YMCA, I suffered a heart attack while swimming laps in the pool. On my second lap, I could not move my arms. I climbed out of the pool myself and got to the hospital. One whole day later, after some three sets of blood work, they confirmed that I had indeed suffered a "myocardial infarction," a fancy term for what every man over 40 fears most, a heart attack. A cardiac catherization confirmed my worst fears. I had to have a quadruple bypass heart procedure right away. The doctor told me that I had "blockage, major blockage."

If it was possible to die of nothing more than devastating disappointment, I would have perished that very afternoon. I had finally allowed myself to believe that I was going to be able to find an escape from this hell I was living. I thought I had finally found the way out, or as I liked to call it, "The Weigh Out." I had been told by doctors my whole life that if I ever needed to have surgery, I would never survive the operation weighing almost 400 pounds. My father was average weight when he had this same procedure and he never fully recovered. I imagined myself scarred drastically, disabled, unable to exercise anymore, unable to lift weights. My dream was over.

I had all these big dumb dreams and goals. I was going to be thin for the first time ever, muscles exploding everywhere, big happy grin, and a dazzling, professionally-done 'after picture' of me. Why did I get this far only to have the rug yanked out from underneath me? I honestly believed that I would never wake up after the surgery.

Well guess what? I did not die. I am alive. Not just breathing-with-a-pulse, going-through-the-motions, waking-up-and-going-to-bed alive, but ALIVE! Shortly after my surgery, my surgeon told my immediate family that if I had not lost that first 90 pounds, he would not have been able to operate on me. He told them, and eventually told me, that he would have given me some medications and sent me home to die in a few weeks. It suddenly became very clear to me why I joined the YMCA that particular Sunday. God had sent me on a mission that day to begin the process to save my own life. How cool is that, anyway? Throughout my whole first year of progress, everyone asked me what finally got me going. They wanted to know what the proverbial last straw was for me. I honestly could not think of one. I thought that living as a morbidly obese person was my destiny. I thought my ship had sailed. I was clueless as to what was motivating me to go through all of this. Well, I got my answer.

My recovery was exceptional. It was record-breakingly fast. In 12 weeks, on New Year's Eve, I climbed back in that lap pool and swam ten laps. It was my way of getting back  on the horse that threw me. I returned to work. I returned to strength training. I began to dream big things again. I started doing aerobics classes. I dyed my hair blond, got blue contact lenses, developed a savage tan, bought a new wardrobe, threw out all my black clothes, and started looking really good. The year following the surgery, I lost another 90 pounds – thanks to my new fitness coach and trainer, David Greenwalt. David is another one of those angels God sent into my life just six weeks before I had my heart attack. David and his *Leanness Lifestyle* organization stuck right with me during my recovery. Very few trainers are willing to take on the responsibility of a 300 pound guy who just had a heart attack and heart surgery. I owe my rapid emotional recovery and the second 90 pounds lost to him. I have lost a whopping total of 180 pounds so far. I am 75 percent of the way to my final goal.

I do not want to be just another guy who lost weight. I want to be a guy who lost weight, turned his life around, reclaimed his health, and accomplished so many things that are just unlikely for a guy who used to weigh almost 400 pounds.

So what am I doing? I joined the National Speakers Association as a candidate level member because I have a story that needs to be told. People need to hear that it is possible. There is hope. I want to be the guy out there giving people that hope. I also started my own business and website. I began studying in June 2002 to become an aerobics instructor. I passed the physical exam and certification process in November 2002.

Two years ago, I could not tie my own shoes and here I am down on the floor being critiqued as I do pushups on my toes and leading a class to my own choreography to be able to teach an aerobics class. I have become a karaoke singer and I love it. I never wanted anyone to notice me before and here I am up on stage singing in front of friends and strangers – and I am good at it! I am a published author. I am writing my own book entitled *The Weigh Out*. I was a guest on the radio in Louisville, Kentucky, for a whole hour, talking about my story. I made a video. I spoke at a cardiology conference in December 2002 in front of 732 people. I parasailed 510 feet over Walt Disney World. I have begun running. I was the featured member in the YMCA magazine last summer, and I was featured in David Greenwalt's book, *The Leanness Lifestyle, Volume 4*. David's book was a big step for me. In his book is a before-picture of me at 359 pounds with no shirt on. This is me coming full circle. Two years ago if you saw a picture of me without a shirt on, it meant one thing. I had to have you killed! Now I show that book to everybody. You know why? Because that is in my past and my past does not dictate my future.

I still do not know the whole reason for my ability to change my life at this late stage in my life. There is still another reason for me to be able to accomplish all these things. I know God is preparing me for a greater good. Just like my inability to explain my first year's progress at the time, the true reason for my success is yet to be revealed to me.

Rekindling With
The Front Porch Approach

- Van Carpenter, The Front Porch Philosopher -

*I*magine for a moment that you have been magically transported and are now sitting either on the front porch of a house in your old neighborhood, a vacation get-away at the beach, or perhaps a rustic cabin porch overlooking the mountains. Use your own magical porch experience – wherever you have had an opportunity to sit on a porch. What do you remember? What beauty do you see? Do you hear laughing? How do you feel? The answers to these questions are as varied as the diverse climes where these porches exist and the persons who sit there. But, one thing is for sure, your porch experience was likely a very positive experience filled with an appreciation of nature, reflection on good times, and a time of relaxing and sharing with others.

How can we possibly relate your personal experience on the porch when we talk about rekindling the human spirit? Using the acronym **FRONT**, I hope to have you recall pleasant memories and values from your past porch experience and relate how that experience might help you to rekindle your own spirit today:

F – Porches were a place where Families gathered and talked about everything. It was a Familiar, Fun and Family place. People were able to Focus on things that mattered most to them.

R – Porches were and are a great place for **Relax-ation**, **Retreat** and **Reflection**. Whether it is with that cup of steaming coffee on a beautiful spring morning or **Relaxing** after work, catching a gentle breeze – one had time to pause, be by yourself, **Reflect** on things and **Refine** your solutions.

O – A porch is of necessity an **Open** place. **Open** to the beauty of nature. **Open** to friends and neigh-bors to visit. **Open** to sharing with others and a place where **Open** communication occurred among the generations.

N – Porches were a place for **Neighbors** and pro-vided an eye on the **Neighborhood**. Porches provided a ready platform for community issues or just to visit and catch up with your **Neighbor**. When people sat on their porches – day or night – the community was a safer place. People kept an eye out for their **Neighbors** and **Neighborhood**. With people sitting on their porches, children played easily, adults carried on conversations two or three houses down, and the only thing you had to worry about were mosquitoes.

T – **Talking**, **Thinking**, **Telling** are all easy on the porch. Whether it was **Talking** with friends or family, there was always some kind of issue-based discussion happening on the front porch. More often than not, those discussions would lead to **Telling** humorous stories about life, present and past. Laughter was an ever-present friend on the porch. And if you happen to be solo on the front porch or merely observing the crowd, there was always a lot of Thinking that could be done about a myriad of subjects from romance to finance.

How would you like to embrace these positive **FRONT** porch experiences and values, and start living your life in the same way? What I am suggesting is that you adopt a "Front Porch Approach" to planning and living your life on purpose – a purposeful life that is balanced and full of peace, joy and humor, and in service to others.

My *Front Porch Approach* is built on five basic tenets that are summed up (you guessed it – in another acronym) in the word **PORCH**. This framework will help you to examine and set goals for everything from life's issues to specific tasks at work. Go ahead. Think of something you have been hoping to accomplish in your life or work. See if this Front Porch Approach can help you organize your direction and actions toward that goal.

P-Purpose

Determine and deal with your purpose in life. Who am I really? What was I meant to do? And the important question – am I living a life FULL of purpose – on purpose? Or, how does this challenge or task relate to my life's purpose? Will it be in sync with my purpose or possibly be a detriment?

O-Openness

Are you OPEN to the possibilities that life can bring you? Are you expectant, observant, available, interactive and open to all the potential that exists around you? Are you like an open porch? Open yourself up to success, power, peace or whatever it is you desire.

R-Reflection

STOP and reflect on your blessings and your trials. Too often, we get so busy in the actual "doing" that we stop "being" the person we uniquely are. A period of reflection or examination, based in purpose, can help us refine and renew our life's goals, or clarify directions for a project or task. With a clear direction and purpose, it is a lot easier to forge ahead successfully in life or on your project.

C-Communication

Our words have power. They can either create or destroy. What do you need to say and communicate to others, as well as to yourself, to best support your new goals or direction? How do you garner support from others and create lasting relationships through effective communication? Communication is most effective when you can involve others in your life and work.

H-Humor

Humor is the attitude through which we filter our perceptions of this life. Your life is full of both blessings and curses, of positive and negative circumstances. The difference in the quality of your life is dictated by how you react to these circumstances. As someone once said, your attitude determines your altitude. It is vitally important to have and develop your sense of humor to help you live and enjoy your life (not just joke about it). Humor is an active tactic to keep us physically, mentally and spiritually healthy. Humor is the best help for the serious business of life.

In closing, let me encourage you to stop being locked up in your mental and physical homes. Come sit on the porch a spell (even if it's only in your mind) and start embracing the *Front Porch Approach* of purposeful living, openness, reflection, communication and humor. Embrace the wisdom and joy of porch thinking and living. Rekindle your spirit and share your unique person with others around you. Pretty soon, you will have a lot of neighbors and friends doing the same thing. Focus on your *Front Porch Approach.* When you do, I feel certain you will be better prepared to take action daily on matters that will make this a better world for all of us.

And just think – it all started on the front porch.

Passion

- Alton Jamison -

Is there anything in your life that keeps you awake at night?
Is there anything in your life that gets you up early in the day?
Is there anything in your life that just *feels right*?
Is there anything in your life that pushes the doubt away?

When you can no longer answer these questions,
    you have lost your passion;
When you can no longer find a reason to stay up late
    or wake up early, you have lost your passion;
When you can no longer find that *something* inside of you
    that just *feels right*, you have lost your passion;
When you can no longer push the regret and doubt away,
    you have lost your passion.

Passion is the driving force in each of us to be great;
Passion is what separates a dream from a reality;
Passion is what can turn a small idea into a magnificent invention;
Passion is the nucleus of our soul that keeps us reaching for more.

The hours may have passed and the day may be getting late,
    but don't lose your passion to reach your dreams;
The years have flown by and age is against you,
    but don't lose your passion to make a difference in society;
The mistakes are many and the regrets overflow,
    but don't lose your passion to keep on fighting;
The cares of life may be weighing you down and the burdens are
    on your back, but don't lose your passion to get up and try again.

If you feel that everything has been lost and you have
    nothing left to give...
If you cannot seem to find your way amongst the clouds of life...
If you feel that your ship of opportunity is sinking...
If you can no longer see the vision...

Once again find your passion and it will be your guide.

Choice Is Always An Option

- Billy Arcement, MEd -

*H*ow do you feel about your life? Is it productive? Do you consistently reach the milestones you so vividly imagine in your mind's eye? Do you have the commitment to continue working on your current goals or do you feel burned out and stagnated?

We Can Choose

The beauty of life is that no matter where we find ourselves at any given moment, we always have the choice to move in a different direction and reposition ourselves. By conducting a thorough examination of our past activities, readjusting our tactics and implementing the necessary changes to improve our results, we can reach the milestones of our life. It's never too late to start over.

Before we can successfully begin to move toward our destination of choice, we must build a self-awareness of our weaknesses – the lid on our success jar that stops our progress.

We all bring strength to the table of opportunity. Likewise, we all have weaknesses which, if not corrected, will diminish our ability to maximize and capture the opportunities of life. People who are successful focus on and use their strengths, while surrounding themselves with people who help them overcome their weaknesses. This creates a win-win partnership.

Your Defining Moment

A defining moment in your life is when you clearly recognize your weaknesses and take action to reduce their impact on your business and personal life. Find your own personal support group to help you bridge the gap between failure and success, and you are well on your way. This idea has value no matter what the situation. Capture the defining moment in your life by being big enough to admit where you need help. When you do, you will find many who are willing to support you. This decision can be the difference between reaching your destination or entirely missing your ride.

Ten Ideas To Turn Failure Into Success

➤ *Start with a vision.* Humans are blessed with the ability to think about and visualize future events. We use our imagination to see possibilities. The more clearly we can visualize events, the higher the probability that they will come to fruition. All success begins with a vision. Use the power of your mind to clearly see yourself achieving your visions. This practice develops the emotional side as well. Vivid imagery not only produces the "picture" of success, but the feelings associated with it as well.

What visions do you carry in your mind? How vividly are you using your imagination to "see" yourself in possession of your dreams? Begin to use this unique gift in a positive way. Build a vision of what you want to be, have, or do. That is the starting point for all successful activities.

➤ *To win, you must expect to win.* Once we imagine our future, we must wrap that vision with a belief system that encourages us to fulfill the vision. Those who struggle with life have lost their ability to believe things will ever be different. They focus more on the possibilities of failure than on the potential of success. They fail to realize the truth that every day offers another opportunity to change their circumstance. We must see and believe to achieve!

➤ *We are surrounded by opportunity.* When speaking to audiences about the opportunities life offers, I often equate it to a merry-go-round ride I experienced as a youngster. Next to the merry-go-round was a pole on which was attached a brass ring. As we circled on the ride, we could lean over and reach out to grab a brass ring. If we were successful, we received a free ride. In many ways, life is very similar to that merry-go-round ride. As we move through each day of our life (one circle on the merry-go-round), opportunities (brass rings) are all around us. All we have to do is recognize them as brass rings and reach out to grab them. But like many of the children riding in my day, we fear reaching out to capture the brass ring. Low achievers are content to ride rather than undertake the risk associated with reaching for the brass ring. To truly understand success, we must realize that capturing opportunity demands risk. Are you a risk taker or a safe rider?

➤ *Enjoy what you do or do something else.* Low achievers usually don't like to work or don't like the work they are doing. It's a no-brainer to understand that those who don't want to work will never prosper. For those who work, it is critically important that their work be a joyful experience. Life is too short to work at a miserable job. Look for ways to make your work interesting or enhance your skills to improve your job opportunities.

The critical factor one must understand when searching for a career choice is to match skills and talents to the job requirements. The closer the match, the more enjoyable the work experience will be. Do you have an appreciation of the strengths in your skill and talent arsenal? Do you look for ways to use those assets in your current career? Do you know which careers would best fit your talents and skills?

➤ *Your success depends on other people.* No one is an island. We must interact with and receive the support of others. Build a network of friends in your industry, community, and the world. Identify those who can help advance your career and seek to build a strong relationship with them. Don't let this relationship function as a one-way pipeline. Be willing to reciprocate help when possible. Remember, it is only in giving that we receive. The more people you know, the more opportunity you have to find a resource in times of need. Hang around people who are successful and possess a sound value system. Get to know people of achievement. Listen to their words, watch their actions, then apply what works for you. What kind of friends do you now have? What do you have to offer others that would make someone want to build a supportive relationship with you?

➤ *If you don't ask, you will rarely receive.* I attended a conference at which noted author and business consultant, Dr. Tom Peters, spoke. After his session, I stood in line to purchase his latest book. As I was waiting to get the book autographed, a thought crossed my mind. When I reached Peters, I told him that I would be willing to read his book if he would be kind enough to read mine. He promptly gave me his address and promised to do so. I don't know if he ever actually read my book., but how many of you have sent your autographed book to Tom Peters? If you never ask, you will rarely receive. Are you asking?

➤ *You become like your environment.* Not satisfied where you are? Look around. The power of your environment will either be your albatross or your springboard to success. Start by thinking about and examining your friendships. Please understand that it is better to have no friends at all than just one of the wrong kind of friend. People born to poverty generally stay that way because they fail to change their environment or friends. What role has your environment and choice of friends played in your success or failure to achieve? Open your eyes and take a long, serious look. This is not the time to go blind!

➢ *Your thinking is critical.* Earl Nightingale once said, "We become what we think about." What do you spend most of your time thinking about – success or failure? Our thinking ultimately helps develop our beliefs. Our beliefs in turn control the way we act. Our actions produce the results we get from our efforts. Finally, it is our results that define whether we have succeeded or failed. So – what are you thinking about all day long?

➢ *Become a perpetual learner.* Successful people understand that school is never out. Every day, they seek new ideas to help them advance toward their dreams. They are hungry for information and feed on knowledge. Then they take the new knowledge and use it to enhance their actions and results. They read books and magazine articles, attend seminars, listen to tapes while driving, and build relationships with successful people. They spend very little time watching television.

Try this idea to transform your career and life. Commit time to read one book a month for the next year, with a focus on career and self-improvement topics. Are you ready for such a growth effort? Are you willing to make such a choice?

➢ *Everyone is entitled to success.* Let me close by assuring you that you deserve to reach your dreams and experience success. No matter where you began your life's journey, you can reach the destination of your choice. The first requirement is that you make the choice. Have you?

Awakened

Dance in the Light

- Sylvia Gay Scott -

It is wonderful to be able to open your eyes in the morning.
To see
the day has changed in someway.
Maybe it rained while you in twilight, slept dreaming.
The smell of the moist earth
flowed through your open window
enrapturing your entire room.
As you breathe deeply of the earth's perfume
your body moves silently to the open panes.
You can hear, by their soft platting journey, what is left of the raindrops
as they slip from leaf to leaf on their way to the forest floor.
A woodpecker raps sharply on the soul of a tree,
to find substance in the unity of his life.
One swoop of her powerful wings
carries an owl from the treetops to the dense foliage below,
where landing on an outreaching limb she sleeps.

The day seems so bright, like a reflection of dawn on a crystal lake.
I can hear my breathing, so tranquil and light
as it passes through my body
I feel so much strength in the universe
and find that in this small space of time
the earth is giving me part of itself,
an energy of love
to sustain my spirit and soul.
It is with this remarkable awareness and peaceful submissiveness that,
willingly I give
and take
this moment like no other, holding it precious as it completes me.
As in Love and Companionship, I fly with the being of a gentle spirit,
and light down when at its end.
Realizing its fulfillment,
I embrace this … .
Plant a gentle kiss upon A soul
and softly walk away.

I'm A Real Person
- Bil Holton, Ph.D. -

*E*arl Loomis, in *The Self In Pilgrimage,* tells the story of a little boy who joined his mother and older sister for lunch. After taking the mother's and sister's orders, the waitress addressed the youngster.

"What will you have, young man?"

"I'll order for him," emphasized his mother, who steeled her gaze on the waitress.

Undaunted, the waitress re-addressed the youngster, "Young man, what will you have today?"

"A cheeseburger," the lad whispered.

"Would you like it medium or well done?"

"Well done, please," said the youngster, brightening a bit.

"Would you like mustard, pickles, onions, relish or ketchup?"

In a burst of self-confidence, the boy exclaimed, "The whole works! I want everything."

As the waitress walked away, the lad looked happily at his chaperones.

"Gee, Mom, she thinks I'm a real person."

Do you make snap judgments about others that affect the way you interact with them? What can you change, so everyone you meet says, "Wow! I just got treated like a real person!"

Choosing Freedom

- Ray Miles Rimmer -

*H*ellhole loomed above me, its entrance a window to blue sky 180 feet straight up. The surrounding dimly-lit gray limestone walls curved upwards, overhanging cathedral-like, to that reassuring sunlit opening.

It was the late 60s. My Wingate College buddies and I had one more weekend to seek adventure underground before graduating and joining the real world – Vietnam, careers, families. I contented myself eating lunch at the bottom of the drop, while others explored adjacent horizontal passages. Speleologists had just identified a rare bat species in Hellhole, so we'd be among the last to explore it before it was closed. Since roosting bats can die after being disturbed, I figured one less explorer in this realm of our subterranean winged-mouse friends was just as well. Without human intrusion, bats thrive in caves, in an unchanging environment of constant temperature, away from snow and rain. Forget the saying "Blind as a bat." Bats see well, and in total darkness, their sonar gives them flight and freedom.

Encountering this grand underground chasm and enjoying the spectacular drop into it is what I relished. The rappel had been breathtaking! We placed protective rope pads on the rock lip below our tie-off tree. Rappelling past the ledge, the cavern walls receded. I soon was suspended, like a spider hanging on its web-thread, inside Hellhole's pit. I let the rope slide through my gloved hand as I glided and gently spun deeper into the chamber, landing on breakdown boulders.

A few feet away, our nylon rope hung straight down from the entrance skylight, as if dangling from the roof opening in a darkened, empty Houston Astrodome. I felt the fear all vertical cavers encounter – that "what if …" *What if …*

someone came upon our rope tied to that tree and untied it, as has happened. On a Mexico expedition in 1968, a mushroom-crazed young Arahuac had suddenly unsheathed his machete and whacked through the taut rope, plunging Canadian caver Mary Fish 30-feet down to – luckily – only a broken leg. The next year, I stayed topside to guard the rope.

What if … the rope breaks while I ascend, perhaps abrading through at the lip of the pit, where our rope pad could have shifted. I shuddered to recall poor Marcel Loubens, being hoisted from that cave shaft in the Pyrenees, suddenly plunging to his death when the French Army's winch cable failed. While that very story in Haroun Tazieff's *Caves of Adventure* had inspired me to explore caves, exploration was no death wish. Quite the opposite, caving was an adventure that sharpened the love of life, beauty, and freedom – and all we hold dear.

There was no way to guard our rope from below, and no way that I or my gung-ho friends were going to miss out doing that rappel. Any fears, dangers, and past tragedies always reinforced that we would be doubly careful. We had placed that rope pad, inspected that rope. We had good equipment, and we knew how to use it. Knowledge, experience, and understanding offer a liberating power, a refined judgment, allowing one to live life more fully and freely, and appreciate it. The paradox in gaining that liberation was in "the getting there." I recalled my first rappel, alone, in 1964. I had wrapped the rope twice around my one borrowed carabiner, which I attached to my leather belt – yes, pants belt. I then backed over the edge into a crumbling 19th century pit at Hoover Hill Gold Mine. I enjoyed it, even the foolish hand-over-hand climb back up the rope. I soon understood that I was much "Nearer my God to Thee" than good sense allows.

⌐═╫═╕

Now five years later, we had explored dozens of caves. We'd rappelled and ascended thousands of feet of rope inside them, and on the Carolinas' cliffs, and in abandoned gold mine shafts. In a few more minutes, we'd enjoy a strenuous and dramatic fixed-rope ascent from Hellhole. Then once topside we'd again sigh with thankful relief, breathe easily, laugh, and joke. I relaxed, and laid back on a rock slab that thousands of years before had fallen from that hole above, perhaps first illuminating what might until then have been a totally dark cavern. I guessed the odds in this eon of another such slab falling to sandwich me were less than the odds of a wreck driving home.

Then I saw it, out of the corner of my eye – something in nearby shadows, moving toward me. I sat still as the mouse scurried by. Maybe it was desperately searching for a crumb of food that had fallen from the green world above, or been left by some snacking caver who awaited a turn on the rope. Not much to eat in this sterile world of rock and dirt – even precious little moss.

We'd encountered mice and other surface dwellers in cave entrance areas – the "twilight zone." We'd once been pestered all night by rats as we tried to sleep in the entrance room at a West Virginia cave. But here, at the bottom of this impossible pit – a mouse? Did it tumble in from the sinkhole above? If so, it had miraculously survived a harrowing fall, probably with injuries. Could it climb out, up these overhanging rock walls? I doubted it, but cavers share amazing stories of discovering skeletons, sometimes of long-extinct mammals, a mile or more underground. Skeletons. Poor mouse.

It headed straight for the rope, began climbing, and in seconds was above my reach. I watched dumbfounded as it climbed steadily, up our 7/16-inch lifeline toward that blue window, and freedom. My rope fears returned. What if our rope was salty-sweaty from nervous climbers' hands? What if this mouse likes the smell and taste of our rope? I wished those sharp rodent teeth weren't next to our rope lifeline. Should I shake it off? The fall would likely kill it.

Voices echoed behind me, boots trundling over loose rocks. Larry, Pittman, and Bill approached. I pointed up. "Can you believe that?" The mouse was halfway – nearly a hundred feet straight above. We began to cheer, not too loudly, lest we unnerve it. "Go little mouse! You can do it! You'll make it!" We gave the support and encouragement we always gave each other to this small creature, which possibly sensed a caring tone in our voices.

The tiny gray dot reached the sky's edge, sun glinting off its fur. Then it disappeared. We cheered and laughed, loudly now, relieved that our little hero hadn't lost its grip, and had survived. "You're free now, little mouse! You've made it!" The moment was at once comedy and inspiration. Recall the movie narrator intoning "And Papillon found his freedom ..." as Steve McQueen floated away atop his coconuts, away from the hellish French Guianan prison of Devil's Island. Now our intrepid mouse had found his freedom, hard-won after a very brave climb out of Hellhole.

The laughter and cheers ended. We tied seat harnesses in preparation for our climbs up the rope. Others managed a nervous laugh when I joked that the mouse must be dining on our rope tied around that tree. Eric quickly insisted it must be reveling in a world of sunlight, abundance, food, and color – brilliant greens, sky blues – free at last from that cold, damp prison of a cave. We gazed up at our thin rope, and instantly liked Eric's option better.

Lathrop was about to grab the standing rope to attach his Prusik friction knots, when Tom stopped him. "Don't touch the rope!" We peered up, and there it was, again, a speck of movement at the pit's edge. Then it was back on the rope, and plainly climbing – down. "No, little mouse! Go back!" Had the sunlight, color, fresh breezes and freedom been too great a shock for a creature now accustomed to the constant gray world of the cave? I resisted an urge to shake the rope, to frighten it back up, knowing that a different result was more likely. It descended steadily, soon halfway, then nearing us. At about knee height, it leaped off the rope, and silently scampered back into the dim recesses of a cave that Virginia's European settlers named Hellhole.

Maybe our little starved mouse's bones remain there. But just maybe that little wingless bat and high climber was another endangered species we didn't recognize. Maybe – with no humans around to marvel at its exploits – it playfully scaled those towering stone walls often. And maybe its progeny are still there. They still play similar tricks on rare bat scientists, just as they did us. Imagine the resident cave mice chuckling in their darkness – or above, in sunlit woods – after human visitors have left nature's inspiring domains, underground and above, for very different man-made worlds – for the heavens, hells, prisons, and freedoms of our own creation, definition, perception, and ultimately, our own choosing.

Who's Listening?

- Susan E. Greene -

*A*n executive group in Oakland was in trouble. *They were being wrenched apart because they hadn't had the most important conversation.*

To practice the skills I'd covered that morning facilitating the 'Power of Candor' program, I invited them to talk about anything that was on their minds or hearts but hadn't been willing to bring up. Next thing I knew, the group was in chaos heading into total oblivion.

It was perfect! They were finally dealing with issues that had been subtly sabotaging them for months. Although it was time for me to catch the plane from San Francisco to Houston, they pleaded with me to help them through the discussion. After 17 years facilitating groups, I've learned that if it shows up … handle it.And so, I agreed.

After everyone had a chance to be heard, they managed to go from congeniality to chaos to mutuality to solidarity in just a short time. Wow! Every participant embraced the new information, used the tools effectively and felt better for taking the risk.

Oakland is 60 minutes away from the San Francisco airport. It's 2:15 p.m. and the plane departs at 3:30 p.m. You do the math. To make things worse, I didn't have a map. I'd planned time to have a quick lunch with the group, get directions, drive to the airport, return the rental car and arrive 30 minutes early. Another plan gone awry!

It seems that every day, plans change. Is it a challenge? Sandra Yancey, CEO, eWomenNetwork, says: "Take the word challenge and cross out the three middle letters – you now have change."

So plans change. What I know is that it'll come together easily if I get out of the way. Since I was willing to continue as needed, I knew that God, Jesus, the angels, the Universe or whatever you call the Divine, would stay with me.

This is FAITH. This trusting that I am in the right place at the right moment is how I choose to live – and be there without drama.

Getting directions from the parking garage attendant, I head towards San Francisco. I consciously choose not to look at the clock. I'm listening – I mean intently listening – to my guidance system – not the one Hertz puts in their cars, but the internal one we all have. It's our personal inner guidance, the voice that keeps us on track if we listen. How do the geese know to fly south for the winter? How do pigeons find their home? How do the Alaskan salmon know to swim up the river for breeding? We all have inner guidance systems.

After crossing the Oakland Bridge and heading south towards the airport, I see the San Marino exit for rental car returns. Oops! This is San Marino Freeway – NOT San Marino Boulevard! Turning around means traversing two freeways before I could get to the rental car exit. By that time the plane would have departed. What do I do now? Angels help!!!

Immediately I hear, "Take the first exit. Turn left." No signs for the airport. "Go down three blocks and when you get behind the white truck follow it." Whoa … there is a white truck. Still there are no signs about any airport facilities, parking, NOTHING. I don't panic. The voice continues giving directions. About ten minutes later I'm pulling into the back of the car rental facility.

Leaving the car, I run to the shuttle bus. Thank heavens for quick check out. As I approach airport security, another lane opens up, and I arrive at the gate just as they announce first class passengers boarding. *They kept my seat!*. In just a few minutes I was sitting on the plane, which departed at 3:30 p.m.

You're probably asking how this is possible. It's really very simple. As Geoffrey Hoppe says, "You dance with the one who shows up at the door." Listen to the inner voice *and* trust it explicitly. For me, I can hear it. Some perceive with images, others with sensations. We all have our own particular way of expressing our innate wisdom.

Trust and follow through without creating drama. When I was a *drama mama,* it didn't come together as easily. The trust wasn't there nor could I perceive the messages.

Another example: Jim and I were preparing our honeymoon in Ruidoso, New Mexico. I went to Ruidoso's website and discovered Shadow Mountain Lodge in Upper Canyon. They had a honeymoon cabin, Spurs and Lace. The name says it all. It was gorgeous. The pictures indicated there was a fireplace with candles on the mantle for leisurely breakfasts and cozy evenings. There was a large Jacuzzi with three huge candle pillars on the floor that created the most amazing glow. Any woman would feel beautiful in that setting. The canopy bed had lots of pillows and a down comforter. The ample couch and chairs looked comfy. The spacious bright kitchen was delightful with full-sized appliances. The ceilings were tall, with high windows allowing lots of light. You could even watch the sunrise, cozily tucked in bed. The view of the trees from the porch and balcony windows looked lovely, even if it would be too cold to enjoy sitting outside in November. We'd found the perfect place for our honeymoon – until I saw the price. Oh well, maybe for our 25th anniversary!

I searched many different cabins, homes, inns and condos, finally selecting a large room back at Shadow Mountain Lodge. No Jacuzzi and the living area smaller. The view was limited, but it fit our budget easily.

Reservations were made for the trip, including Thanksgiving dinner when we arrived. Ten days before we left, while busy with Saturday morning chores, that inner voice said, "Call the lodge and ask about Spurs and Lace again – they'll negotiate."

I trust that voice. This time the owner answered the phone. Discovering the Spurs and Lace cabin was available, I asked if he was willing to lower the price since we were coming for a week, not just the holiday. Guess what price he came up with? The top figure of our budget! Yep – we had a delightful honeymoon. What would we have missed if I hadn't made that call?

How many times do you hear a voice, or experience a sudden thought that seems totally unrelated to what you're doing, but is relevant with something else? That's your inner guidance system at work – just like the nudge I got to make that call.

Then sometimes the guidance system is operating and we haven't a clue! For example: The phone rings. My sister Leanne gives us the bad news: Dave, my 43-year-old brother-in-law, had a stroke at work. Had a stroke! Dave climbs mountains, cross country skis, and bicycles across Nova Scotia for fun. The prognosis: he'll probably never walk again. I decided to be there when he came home in his wheel chair.

I immediately made arrangements to fly to Providence and meet my other sister, Katie. The two of us would drive the four-and-a half hours to Leanne's, in time for Dave's homecoming.

Checking in at the airport, the porter announced the flight had already closed. What? I'd allowed the usual 75 minutes from home to check-in when I gave my driver, Pedro, my pick-up time. Somehow I'd miscalculated.

> *Listen to the inner voice and trust it explicitly. For me, I can hear it. Some perceive with images, others with sensations. We all have our own particular way of expressing our innate wisdom.*

At the check-in counter I admitted I'd messed up, then explained why I needed to reach Providence today. I asked if there was any way they could reroute me. I didn't get angry. I wasn't the *drama mama*.

Houston, there is a problem. Flights to Newark were iffy. Thunderstorms were moving into the area later that day. Would the flight be able to land? Would connecting flights to Providence depart? It didn't look good.

Choosing the next option, I flew to Cleveland, then waited eight hours for the connection to Providence. Still not irritated … going with the flow. Trusting I'm in the right place at the right time.

I was leaving messages everywhere, telling Katie the arrival was at 11:30 p.m., not 3:20 p.m. No point getting frustrated. Instead, I enjoyed the quiet to catch up on e-mail, read and be grateful I'd brought the laptop.

At 5:50 p.m., I finally reached Katie. She'd been to the airport and was told my flights were cancelled. Not receiving any messages, she thought I was still in Houston. That's when I found out what had happened with my original flight. Because of a cancelled flight in New York City, the passengers on my original flight were all stranded in Cleveland, with no flight out available. If I had told Pedro the correct time to pick me up, I'd have been stranded in Cleveland too. Instead, I was booked on a flight to Providence.

Isn't this interesting? I hadn't realized that I gave Pedro the wrong pick-up time. Not reacting, I took action. Catching up on my work, as well as getting to our final destination on time, was relatively easy.

How could I not trust and have the faith that we are always in the right place at the right moment? Are you paying attention? Can you trust? Are you listening to your guidance system?

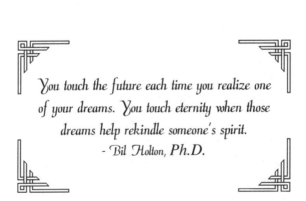

You touch the future each time you realize one
of your dreams. You touch eternity when those
dreams help rekindle someone's spirit.
- Bil Holton, Ph.D.

Reshape Your Mind For a Better Life

- Jeff Davidson, MBA, CMC -

*J*ust as your muscles get flabby and weak when they're not regularly exercised, so does your mind. An out-of-shape mind is a huge obstacle to growing and changing in life. Life is an exciting adventure, and you do not want anything, especially your own mind, to work against you.

Taking Action

The world is full of people who buy self-improvement books, read them cover to cover, and put them on a shelf next to a bunch of other self-improvement books. Meanwhile, their lives continue, no different from before. When people do this, it's often because they're not really thinking about what they're reading. The words flow past their eyes and into their brains, but no substantive thought takes place as a result. Reading can be a useful tool, but it must be used correctly. Be alert and retain the knowledge that you gain from it.

Finding Your Learning Niche

Everyone has different learning styles. While some people prefer self-guided learning, others find that they learn more effectively within some sort of structured educational program. If you're one of those people, then going to college, or going back to college, may be a great way for you to exercise your mind.

What better way exists to get your brain going than through structured learning? You can take non-credit continuing education courses, such as "How To Write A Novel" or "Landscaping for Beginners." You can enroll in courses for credit in an area in which you're interested, such as history or a foreign language, without enrolling as a degree-seeking student. You can enroll in a certification program to gain a new skill. Anything from phlebotomy to paralegal courses are available.

Going Back to College

You could also enroll in a typical undergraduate or graduate degree program. If you're at all interested in taking college courses of any kind, don't hesitate to get in touch with your local institutions of higher education. Virtually all of them have Web sites, which have a complete list of programs and course offerings. Learn what options are available to you and determine whether or not any of them spark your interest.

If you think you're too busy to take any classes, keep in mind that there are more and more colleges offering programs geared toward nontraditional students. Most schools, especially community colleges, offer night courses to fit the schedules of working students.

Some schools have adult degree programs that offer flexible scheduling, distance learning, and individualized curriculum design to accommodate the needs and abilities of adult learners. More colleges are offering courses online, and increasingly schools are offering entire undergraduate and graduate degree programs over the Internet. Going back to school, or going for the first time, may be much easier than you thought.

Many adult students also report that their college education is much more fulfilling and rewarding than the educational experiences they had when they were younger. Older students typically are more responsible and mature, which usually makes them better students. They often are

more diligent in their schoolwork, resulting in less perceived pressure and better grades. They also may find that
they can relate to their instructors more easily than to
younger students, due to the closeness in age. Most people
who go back to school or who begin at a late age are very
glad they did, because now they are wise enough to make
the most out of it.

Reshaping your mind can take place from a seemingly
small action, like reading, or from large milestones, like
returning to college for your degree. Whichever path you
choose, remember that life requires an open, limber mind.
You cannot change your life without changing your way of
thinking.

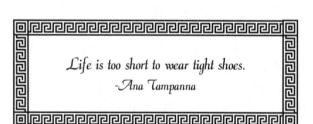

Life is too short to wear tight shoes.
-Ana Tampanna

My Light's Purpose

- Dana C. Foster -

Now that we have stepped into the 21st Century with our blazing technologies, continued quest for wealth, and our ego full of pride from our many accomplishments, the main piece to the puzzle in many lives still remains missing. For the large majority of our populace, the question "Why am I here?" still eludes our conscious thought; yet it attempts to contact our heart and mind almost daily.

Each of us is born with our own certain natural talents and abilities. In the beginning stages of our life, most of us commence an impulsive gravitation toward the discovery of what these talents and abilities are, and what they could potentially mean for our future if we focus on developing them. However, almost simultaneously, our hearts and minds begin to receive negative energy and feedback from everywhere.

Eventually and primarily out of fear, we talk ourselves out of using our hopes, dreams, talents, and abilities to give the world our own authentic maximum contributions. We begin to only seek outside the body guidance and direction. Before long, we have partially bought into someone else's dream, goal or purpose, and begin to use our natural gifts to support them and their cause. As the years roll by, since their purpose doesn't align with ours, we inevitably wind up right back to the very same question: "Why am I here?"

Conversely, there are others whose calling was so strong, they were able to ignore all the rhetoric and pursue the immediate use of their skills. Despite more than a few thousand failed attempts, Thomas Edison knew his talent to create various inventions could not be denied. Harriet Tubman knew her ability to lead others to freedom could not be halted by any laws produced by man. The Wright brothers knew that only the sky was the limit as they fought against all odds to create a flying machine, and now the world has a space station to take mankind even further.

The revolutionary spirit within these individuals caused them to fight the status quo and use their natural talents to bring something absolutely meaningful and important, as well as life altering, to this planet. Just as these folks discovered that the light within them must find a way to shine its purpose, so must you.

So how do you go about finding this Inner Light, revealing its purpose and allowing the cradle of humanity and its people to see it shine? Believe it or not, you have always had the answer. It's the very thing that you are able to do naturally, with little to no effort. You may have kept it hidden or thrown it out for the world to view at some point, only to get hit by the negative forces that surround us.

This may have caused you to hide it even deeper on the inside. Perhaps it is something through which others are making a living, but you don't feel you would be able to do the same, or the time for you has past, or your current job and responsibilities use up all your time. Stop for a moment, and ask yourself: What do I love, enjoy, or feel compelled to do throughout the day that could possibly serve others in some way, shape, form or fashion?

My gift encompassed a desire to entertain. I enjoyed performing so much I would practice almost every day. But I was afraid that I wasn't good enough and the world would not enjoy my actual gift for the globe. As time went on, it no longer mattered what others thought of my abilities, my light was determined to break out into the open – no matter what the results. Now it is my hope that I can continue to cultivate this ability and use it to bring about a positive message that impacts many people in a spiritual way. If you are still searching for your purpose, don't give up, for it is there; just believe in yourself and your God-given gifts and the light will come shining through.

(Artwork by Colleen Fire Thunder)

Using Humor for a Change

- Scott Friedman, CSP -

*W*ith restructurings, takeovers and layoffs sweeping the corporate world, employee insecurity and fear are at record levels. The definition of an optimist in corporate America today is an employee who brings lunch to work. Change has become a daily activity with no end in sight. Anxiety reverberates throughout the entire organization. During these times, corporations need some sort of antidote for stress. Many companies see a dose of humor as a remedy to reduce tension and motivate workers. By coming to our senses of humor, we find truth in the statement that he or she who laughs, lasts.

Does a sense of humor translate into dollars and cents? While the savings won't show up on your balance sheet under comic credits or laugh assets, humor does add an intangible but real benefit.

Humor creates bonds in the workplace. It's the shortest distance between two people. Humor helps establish a feeling of camaraderie and sets the tone for cooperation rather than contention.

To use humor positively at work, people must take themselves lightly, while taking their jobs seriously. Humor is much more than just telling jokes. Humor is the ability to find something funny in your predicament. A comic vision helps people tolerate change in the workplace and get along better with others.

The health of any organization is in direct proportion to that organization's ability to laugh at itself. Many companies are just too darn serious. Their structure and formality inhibit open communications and stifle creativity. If organizations would loosen up a little, they would realize that informality and spontaneity foster open communications and stimulate creativity. What setting is more informal and spontaneous than one with good humor, fun, and play?

Humor is a technique that can be learned, practiced, reinforced, and internalized just like other skills. Where do you start? First, remember that you don't need to be a stand-up comic; you just need to add some spirit to the work environment.

The first ten minutes of the morning set the 'attitude' for the rest of the day, so start light. Here are some ideas:

☺ Start every morning by greeting everyone in the office with a big smile and a hearty hello. They will wonder what you're up to.

☺ Place funny cartoons, appropriate jokes, or post-cards on a company bulletin board. Sign your name with a note saying, "I thought you might enjoy this." Not only are you giving employees an opportunity to laugh at this cartoon or joke, but people will be saying, "I'll be darned, our manager is a real person! What a surprise ... there's a sense of humor in there!"

☺ Sprinkle internal communications with humor. Add a cartoon or funny one-liner to memos and you'll be surprised how many people start reading those little devils.

☺ To get meetings off on a productive foot, serve everyone ice cream or suckers at the start of the meeting. Communication is guaranteed to improve.

☺ Inject humor into meetings. Have a dress-up theme meeting once a quarter. Share 15 minutes of jokes at the start of every meeting.

☺ Have a positive party funded by negative people. Every time someone in the office is caught being negative, they throw a dollar in a positive pot, and once a quarter the pot buys pizza, happy hour, or humor props for the office.

☺ Wear amusing buttons. One executive wears one that says, "Save time, see it my way." Walk into your next meeting with a button that says, "God is watching, give her a good show." Try "Start each day with 'PMS'-a Positive Motivating Smile." Or "If you're too busy to laugh, you're just too busy."

☺ Give rewards for the worst mistake of the week. This will encourage employees to share and learn from their blunders.

☺ Spike your environment. Place positive and appropriate humor props around your office. How about Groucho glasses on your ficus or a red clown nose on your fax machine?

☺ Send out cartoons with your correspondence. Put your clients in a receptive mood before reading proposals.

☺ Have one "call in well" day a year. Instead of calling in sick, you would call up and say, "I'd really love to come to work today, but I just feel too good. Love ya! Bye!"

☺ Keep it light. If an employee is frustrated with a new computer system and can't figure out the manual, a boss may sympathize by saying, "How's that new mystery book you're reading? Can I help?"

☺ Use Aikido to defuse tension. As Tom Crum reminds us in his book, *The Magic of Conflict,* Aikido literally translated means "the way of blending energy." It's blending with the aggressor instead of choosing to be aggressive or defensive.

When an irate client asks, "Have you been incompetent your whole life?" your response could be, "Not yet I haven't." Or when a customer comes in and says, "Okay, who is the idiot in charge here?" say, "I'm head idiot. What can I do for you?" An unexpected non-threatening response absorbs and redirects the anger in a harmless way, without putting the other person down. It may be almost impossible to control others, but you can always control yourself.

A quick warning: Be careful when using Aikido. There is a fine line between positive and negative humor. The first thing to do is ask yourself the question, "Where am I coming from?" If you're coming from a hostile place, it could very well be reflected in your humor, for humor mirrors the truth. Anger or bitterness many times comes out as sarcasm or humor with a biting, caustic edge. You do more harm than if you had said nothing at all.

The most effective humor has its roots in kindliness and affection. The highest form of laughter is to laugh at yourself; the lowest is to laugh at someone else. Making fun of yourself creates instant rapport and creates bonds with workers.

One executive was quoted as saying, "There are two ways to develop self-esteem at the office. The first is to share positive humor, and the second is to take all mirrors out of the washrooms."

A healthy sense of life's absurdities can help us forget our problems and put a smile on our faces. With humor we can sit back, detach ourselves from the situation, and laugh at ourselves for becoming so reactive at life's afflictions. And we can ask ourselves, "Why am I taking life so seriously?" It's not permanent. No one gets out of it alive anyway. In a hundred years, what difference will it make anyway?. So lighten up! If a tornado blows off your roof, be like the guy who put up a sign saying, "Open House Today."

Laughter is contagious –
Why not infect the whole company?

Mya

- Cher Holton -

On October 30, 1999, we were given the gift of becoming grandparents with the birth of Mya Elizabeth Holton. As her first Christmas approached, we wanted to do something very special. My husband, Bil, came up with the unique idea of creating a Time Capsule for her, with pictures and letters from all her family members, giving her words of love, wisdom and hope as we entered the year 2000. When she is old enough, she will be able to look back and read our wishes for her as she entered this world.

Here is part of my message – a poem I wrote for Mya:

Today I held you, my first grandchild, in my arms –
And my whole world shifted in place.
As I stared with wonder at your beautiful, trusting, innocent face
All of a sudden it mattered ...

It mattered that parents can no longer afford to be home with their children,
That they are required to work longer and harder than ever before;
It mattered that we are replacing all our parks with shopping malls, developments and office buildings;
That we are using tax money for jails instead of schools;
That we're waging a war on drugs and crime –
And the good guys are losing.

As I watched you – a tiny bundle of joy,
I wanted to wrap my arms around you
    And promise that you would always be safe –

But I couldn't make that promise.

I wanted to promise that you would always be
    happy and successful,
    And you would always have all the resources
    you'd need
    To achieve your dreams –

But again, these were promises I knew I could
    not guarantee.
Gazing into your innocent, tender, awesome face
    – my first granddaughter –
All I could promise you was that you would
    always be cherished –
That God was in charge –
    That we would always love you.

And with every fiber of my being,
    I will make the choices in my life to keep that
    promise to you –
And, by knowing you are so loved and
    cherished,
All the other promises are yours to claim.

Heart-Sense: In Service to Others

- Janet Holliday-Cashwell, Ed.D. -

When was the last time something tugged at your heart strings? Perhaps it was the birth of your first child, the marriage of your youngest, or the loss of someone dear. Both gain and loss leave lasting imprints on our hearts, allowing sweetness and sadness to commingle in an odd sort of way. Sometimes, memories are so sweet our hearts are filled to bursting. At other times, there are life events that cause us to consider shutting down *el corazon* altogether, not offering it up for any further activity that will scar it again – ever.

There are many situations in life that shape our heart's capacity to love, to laugh, to give of ourselves to others. Sometimes, natural tragedies propel us forward to reach out to others. Sometimes, these same events cause us to withdraw from the world and just be thankful we are not in the predicament. Maybe the situation seems too hard for us to address. Maybe we simply don't know what to say, what to do, or how to start. Just maybe we need to begin strength-training the most vital element of our emotional and spiritual being: our heart-sense.

Life provides ample opportunities in which to focus on making connection to others in need. For many, an economic downturn causes individuals to reassess spiritual toughness as well as financial position, sometimes for the very first time. Impending layoffs and a shortage of jobs have wreaked havoc on many people – on their lives, their livelihoods, their very spirits. What's more, the personal turmoil has touched both those who are processed out through downsizing as well as those who remain in the workplace to carry on in the wake of having lost employees, co-workers, friends.

As a Human Resources manager by profession, I've interfaced with hundreds of employees in the throes of downsizing, rightsizing, and quite honestly, incising. While employee cuts within the company body usually heal, the incisions always leave a scar – on those who leave and those left behind. The phenomenon often leaves remaining employees sleepless, jittery, and at a loss for words – emotionally paralyzed and unable to interact with former co-workers.

There have been times when this phenomenon has left me in the same physical and mental state, but my professional responsibility is to support impacted employees. As a result, I now have a treasure case of friendships I could not have acquired any other way. Some of the richest and most rewarding professional and personal relationships I now enjoy were born of the necessity to interface with employees during difficult professional and personal experiences. Having held hands, literally, with those experiencing trauma in life has required me to exercise heart-sense. Doing so has been emotionally costly for me at times. The payback has far exceeded the cost, however, for the opportunities have renewed and expanded my capacity for heart-sense. My walk with those in unfortunate circumstances has taught me more about my own personal walk. The experience has truly been spiritually rewarding.

Because I have been involved in separation activity for so long, one of my longtime co-workers rather innocently nicknamed me the "Angel of Death." The description stuck, and employees quickly sensed that if I showed up on their floor, bad news was probably not far behind. Once in a while, I still hear the Grim Reaper reference. As a result, I never wear black when I take part in employee separation meetings.

No one willingly signs on to be the "bearer of bad news." Most individuals who work in this capacity don't have degrees in psychology, they aren't found on the best-selling self-help author lists, nor do they possess some Certificate of Know-How to deal with these situations. What they do have is a passion for service to others and the compassion that allows them to perform that service. They have heart-sense.

Losing one's job, taking a demotion because there is no alternative, being out of work with or without separation pay – all of these certainly qualify for the "tough times" category. Any individual who weathers these or any other storms of life emerges transformed, sometimes for the better, sometimes not. What doesn't kill us makes us stronger. What makes us stronger gives us greater capacity for whatever life may present to us.

> *There are many situations in life that shape our heart's capacity to love, to laugh, to give of ourselves to others.*

While there is no "right" thing to say, no "proper" way for an impacted individual to react, we quickly learn that working with employees in the downsize mode requires one basic life principle: compassion.

Backing away is not an option for a caregiver. More specifically, there is not a shut-off valve in the chamber where heart-sense resides. "To the world you might be one person; to one person you might be the world," a friend's email tag reminds me each time we talk on-line. That sentiment sums up the emotional bank account from which we must withdraw as we work to rekindle others. The feedback from those in need results in bittersweet deposits made to that account. In turn, that is what rekindles our spirits. Slogging through the bad times – personally or while assisting others – does make us appreciate the good times all the more.

So, what is heart-sense, exactly?

Heart-sense is that virtual inner lining of the most vital organ we possess. It's activated by and maintained through compassion for and service to others. The physical heart signals its wellbeing through a steady, strong rhythmic thump-thump, thump-thump, thump-thump. The sense of heart, where emotion and spirit co-exist, likewise pounds out emotional response and physical action. Created in God's image, we are encoded to be responsive to others. But unlike any other life form, we possess the element of reasoning through choice. If our will reasons not to exercise heart-sense, that component will become rusty, useless, and eventually, non-existent.

Heart-sense is about relating to others on a very basic level. It is about being sensitive to others' needs, determining an appropriate response to those needs, and following through on commitments to others without regard to self-gain. Generally, there are three tactical options when dealing with others: decision, indecision, and no decision. No decision is the most heartless of all. In choosing not to interact, well-intentioned individuals, trying to spare someone else's feelings (or their own), have in fact accomplished just the opposite. And that leaves a void of unsaid thoughts and undemonstrated concern to be filled by the rabid imagination of those affected individuals seeking desperately to bring order and sense into a world that feels anything but orderly.

Recently, a RIF'd employee shared with me an everyday activity that left him feeling like an outcast and unworthy. While at the grocery store, he saw a friend from his former place of employment at the other end of the aisle. Wanting to have conversation with the still-employed friend, he approached the individual. The friend, obviously aware of the former employee's presence, abruptly turned away to shop in another part of the store. The friend did not meet the former co-worker eye-to-eye, nor stay to have just a word of conversation. The separated employee described the incident thus: "I didn't have any fingers or toes falling off, but I felt like a leper."

No need to ponder the excuses behind that kind of reaction. Bottom line, people don't know what to say or how to react. Those who remain employed while observing co-workers being released go through their own loss cycle of feeling guilty for still being employed, with a steady income; there is anger for seeing this happen to a friend as well as a co-worker; there is the nagging, unhappy realization that the additional work must now be picked up by those still employed; and, there is the ever-present unspoken anxiety – if it happened to that individual, it can happen to me.

So how should we respond when we learn a friend, a co-worker, a fellow human being has suffered loss? Take a quantum leap of faith – confidence in our own abilities, openness to the receptiveness of those we strive to help, and most importantly, trust in that Entity far greater than all humankind. Our charge is to help restore those less fortunate.

> *I was hungry and you gave me something to eat.*
> *I was thirsty and you gave me something to drink.*
> *I was a stranger and you invited me in.*
> *I needed clothes and you clothed me.*
> *I was sick and you looked after me.*
> *I was in prison and you visited me.*
> *I tell you the truth, whatever you did*
> * for one of the least of these brothers of mine,*
> *you did for me. (Matt 25: 35-40, NIV)*

There is absolutely nothing unclear about that mission call.

First, we must show concern. Concern takes into account many acts from the simple to the complex. A card, a phone call, a prayer, an e-mail, or a visit lets the individual know that we have heard the news, we care, and we are there for them.

Will we always say the right thing? Probably not. Case in point: Near the end of the visitation at the wake for a friend's relative, my friend approached and asked how I was. Without thinking, I responded, "Dead on my feet." Honestly (and obviously mindlessly) spoken? Yes. Sticking to the basics of greeting etiquette would have served me so much better. In the next instant, I was talking with my mouth full – of tired dogs – as I attempted to change the subject.

Second, we must follow up concern with communication – sincerely asking how someone is doing, not merely as a greeting, but out of genuine concern. Sometimes, depending on one's heart-sense quotient, the conversation is accompanied by an arm around the shoulder, a quick hug, or hand-holding. These nonverbals often convey the compassion that verbals alone cannot. Whether paired with kind words or used solo, they are powerful restorers of others' spirit as well as eagle's wings under our own.

Silence speaks volumes when others need to tell and retell their loss. The old adage of "two ears, one tongue" (for twice the listening and half the talking) really does have merit. Besides, what can you possibly say to the intensely private person who tells you he has a terminal illness and wants your advice on how to tell his manager? What do you tell an employee who says she has a family to support, she's given 20+ years of her life to the company, and right now she feels it's all been for naught? For heaven's sake, how do you express your grief – minimal by comparison as it must be – to that mother and father who have just lost their only child? (There are no words – just tears and hugs and angel whispers.)

These and countless other scenarios fill in the complexity of human relationships, whether it's about companies trying to achieve the 'right' balance between spreadsheet and personnel, or personal relationships in which the world has spun off course. There is no formula, no textbook answer for any of these situations. The response we must give to those among us who are "starting again" must be realistic, yes. But it is equally important that those responses be positive and uplifting. While we will surely employ book sense and common sense in working with those who need assistance, we must apply an even greater measure of heart-sense as well.

Overlay communication with compassion. Put words into action. Compassion is that outward expression of empathetic understanding when we know individuals need reassurance, a spirit lift, some physical assistance, or just pure human contact.

Concern, communication, and compassion are the catalysts for service to others. These actions refire the spark that helps people recharge themselves. There are many paths we might take to minister to the needs of others. At times, no one road is any better than another. There is only one reason we take any direction: we care, plain and simple.

※

Dear Lord,

I am the vessel you chose to assist someone somewhere today. Let me be attentive and attuned to that person's needs. Instruct me in what to say, what actions to take, and how to extend my heart as well as my hand. This I ask in Your name and in Your will,

Amen.

A Lesson From Basketball

- Ted Hurwitz -

I learned my life lesson as a young college basketball player sitting on the bench, never getting into the game. I sulked and blamed the coach, believing I was the best player on the team.

Then I noticed that one of the other players got into each game for a few minutes, even though I was a much better player than he was. I also noticed that he was always positive, rooting aloud for the team when he was sitting on the bench. I thought I would try it. Sure enough, I started to get some time in the game, and by mid season, I worked my way up to being the first substitute.

Another thing I noticed: if one of the guards missed two shots in a row, I would be put into the game for that person. So whenever one of them would take a shot, I found myself saying (in my mind, of course), "Miss, miss!" Aloud I was rooting for them, and when they missed, I'd reassure them by saying, "That's okay, you'll make the next one." However, when they took another shot, I would think, "Miss, miss!" Sure enough, if they missed that second shot I was in the game.

As the season progressed I experienced a major shift in my thinking. As I became more positive, I found I was no longer thinking "Miss, miss!" Instead, I was rooting hard and loud, hoping they would make every shot. You may call it coincidence, but as I became more positive, putting my whole self into rooting for the team, I became a better player, and earned much more playing time on the floor!

What I took away from this is that "people hear what you say and see what you do, but they cannot read your mind." If you say and do the right thing, your mind will eventually follow suit. As your mind becomes more positive and focused, you will have a happier, healthier and more enriching life. So, take a look at what you are thinking, and strengthen your winning thoughts!

The Power Of Words:
From the Impossible Dream to Living the Life!
- Theresa Behenna -

*H*ave you ever opened your mouth, inserted both feet and wished you could disappear from the face of the earth? Have you ever said something you wish you'd thought out before allowing your tongue to wag within hearing distance of another? Do you ever think about how words can powerfully impact our lives?

Twenty years ago I was playing the piano in the lovely Shangri-La Hotel in Singapore. As a professional musician from Australia, I had been travelling around the world for several years and I dreamed of going to America. There was just one big problem. I didn't think I was good enough. I thought I was just an "okay" pianist.

The most popular song in Singapore at that time was "Don't Cry For Me Argentina" by Andrew Lloyd Webber. People would request this song up to five times a night! One particular evening the piano lounge was packed with 150 people and I was playing the song for the fourth time, by request. I was so totally bored I wasn't paying any attention to anyone or anything. Much to my surprise, at the end of the song the entire room burst out into thunderous applause. Delighted at the response and riding on the moment, I quickly segued into the next song "If I Were A Rich Man," and now that everyone's attention was on the music, the audience clapped along in tempo, creating a lively, exciting atmosphere. I was on a roll. This was MY time to shine! I knew I had them in the palm of my hand and I wanted to enjoy every minute of it!

Much to my annoyance, a man walked up to the piano and interrupted my playing as he continued with what seemed like a non-ending one-sided conversation about my work. He babbled on about how nice it was to hear Argentina played so well and was that my own arrangement, yada, yada yada.

I felt extremely irritated that I was losing my momentum with the audience. This man was stealing my moment in the spotlight by acting like a dingleberry – and one whom I believed needed a new pick-up line. Finally I burst out in good old Aussie style, "Look Mate, can't you see I'm busy?"

He gave me a quizzical look and said: "I'm awfully sorry. I let my enthusiasm run away with me. Let me introduce myself. My name is Andrew Lloyd Webber. Who are you?"

☙—❧

Lesson: Words matter. Words change lives. Andrew Lloyd Webber's few words of praise changed my life forever and bought me to America.

When was the last time you gave a few words of encouragement to your child, your partner, a friend, your employee or a co-worker? Try it. You may never realize the tremendous difference YOU can make.

A New View

- Christina W. Giles -

I've never considered myself a "religious" person. Of course, that term is a very personal one and would be defined differently by each of us.

I believe I have attempted to live my life by the Golden Rule: *Do unto others as you would have them do unto you.*

Although I have not embraced a formal, organized religion since I was in my early 20's, I do believe in a higher being and also believe that we were created by that higher being. We are provided with whatever abilities we are born with and can achieve/develop during our lifetime – the rest is up to us. I have never understood death, still have many unanswered questions and unfortunately lack a strong belief or conviction that might help me through a difficult loss.

All these words are basically to say, when I suffer from the death of a friend or loved one, I often feel so lost, confused and frightened. I try to push those feelings away and get back into the world of the living.

I lost my mother a year ago and I've found it increasingly difficult to really get back "into the living." Mom and I had our issues; she was a difficult person at times, as we all are. She had some very strong feelings and opinions, and cared a lot about people – her family in particular. We went through a very difficult time with her. She suffered two strokes, with a third one that brought on her death.

While going through her papers, I found a note she had written quite a long time ago to all her family members, containing a poem she wanted us to read at the time of her death. I enclosed that poem with notes to many of her dear friends, informing them of her death. Her address book contained that poem, a quote from Edith Wharton and the poem

Renascence by Edna St. Vincent Millay. I remember reading and studying the poem *Renascence* when I was in high school and liking it so much I brought it home to show Mom and discuss with her. She evidently liked it too, and typed it up to keep in her address book for over 40 years!

My mother was dedicated to her children, and after we added to the family, to her grandchildren. She was very involved in our lives and our children's lives and was very proud of all of us. She was a strong and independent person, just like *her* mother. My grandmother was one of the first truly independent women I ever knew. She was definitely way before her time in her thoughts and beliefs. We were – and still are – a family of very strong women.

I enjoyed seeing my mother relate to my children, and they enjoyed knowing they had a grandmother (Nana) who loved them dearly and who was extremely proud of everything they accomplished. High school and college graduations were great cause for celebration, and we were all looking forward to the next step in their lives: marriage and children. Luckily, Mom was able to attend my son's wedding even though she had suffered one stroke. She had recuperated enough to be able to walk and travel with assistance. A few months later, Mom had her second stroke which paralyzed her on one side. The next year, on November 6, she died.

My daughter had been dating the same young man for several years and Mom was always asking when they were going to get married. Christmas morning, 5:00 a.m. to be exact, the month after my mother passed away, my daughter called to tell me she had received her engagement ring. She was so excited and asked me to come over and be with her, because after her fiancé had proposed, he had to return to finish his night shift as a police officer. My immediate thoughts went to my mother. I cried to think how happy she would have been and how sad it was that she wasn't going to be with us throughout the harried but exciting time of planning a wedding. I pulled myself together though, and started getting dressed, determined to go and be with my daughter without showing the sadness I was feeling.

As I drove out of my driveway, the sun was just beginning to rise. Brilliant colors burst through the clouds – there was pink and yellow and some gray, but the pinks and yellows were vibrant. I experienced déjà vu – a mental image appeared – a picture in a textbook of mine from English 101 – the page with the poem *Renascence* on it – and at that moment I knew Mom was with us, she knew my daughter had gotten engaged, and she was going to share in our happiness.

The wedding took place on December 28. I knew it was going to be a difficult day for me, happy yet sad. There were many people all over the house: bridesmaids, fathers, stepparents, brother, sister and family – much confusion, but no Mom for me. Just as my daughter was readying to enter the limousine for the ride to the church, she called to me and asked for her purse. I told her she didn't need her purse, she wasn't going to be able to carry it or keep it in the car. But she didn't want her purse. She wanted what was *in* her purse – Nana's bracelet. She wasn't going to leave without wearing Nana's bracelet. That caused the tears to start for me, but again, I knew Nana was here with us.

I'm still not sure what my beliefs are concerning an afterlife, but I think I feel much stronger about the fact that loved ones stay with us, one way or another; if we become observant and sensitive to our surroundings, we will feel them or experience something that will awaken a memory, and we will know they are still there, somewhere, perhaps in a different form, but still there.

The poem, *Renascence,* is too long to quote here, but I encourage you to read it. I would like to share the poem Mom sent to us and the quote she kept in her address book.

They both say a lot about who she was, and are a way to keep her with us. Perhaps they will help you in time of need:

"In spite of illness, even in spite of the archenemy sorrow, one can remain alive long past the usual date of disintegration if one is unafraid of change, insatiable in intellectual curiosity, interested in big things and happy in small ways."
                                                    –Edith Wharton

To Those I Love
If I should ever leave you, whom I love
To go along the Silent Way, grieve not,
Nor speak of me with tears, but laugh and
Talk of me as if I were beside you there,
(I'd come – I'd come, could I but find a way!)
But would not tears and grief be barriers?
And when you hear a song or see a bird I loved,
* please do not let the thought of me be sad ...*
For I am loving you just as I always have ...
You were so good to me!
There are so many things I wanted still to do –
So many things to say to you ... Remember that I did not fear ...
It was just leaving you that was so hard to face
We cannot see beyond ... but this I know;
I loved you so – t'was heaven here with you!
                                        –Isla Paschal Richardson

I would like to dedicate this story to my nieces, Cara and Lisa Ciccone. Unfortunately they will not have Nana in person at their high school and college graduations or weddings, but I want them to know she will be with them.

I also want to dedicate this to my granddaughter to be, Elli Christina Wiggins. Her middle name is Nana's name – I hope she will grow up to become a strong and independent woman, as was her great grandmother.

Burned Out!

- Sarah Starr -

Burned out!
Shut down!
Hung up!
Tightly wound!

Gotta get
Off this space!
Move on to
A better place!

Clouds are gone!
Sun is out!
Feeling better!
There's no doubt!

Spirit's strong!
Here I come!
Look out world!
Life goes on!

The CEO's Seeds

- Bil Holton, Ph.D. -

CEO of a large multi-national company was growing old and knew it was time to choose a successor. Instead of choosing one of his direct reports, he decided to include all of his managers and supervisors. He scheduled a special meeting and announced his decision:

"It is time for me to retire, so I have decided that my successor will come from one of you. I have already spoken to my direct reports who, although capable, do not have the time and experience to make them the only candidates for my job next year."

The managers were shocked.

"I am going to give each one of you a seed today," he continued. "One very special seed. All of you have the same assignment. I want you to plant the seed, water it and care for it. We'll meet back here in the conference room one year from today. Bring what you have grown from that one seed. I will then judge what you have planted. The quality of your product will help me determine who among you will be the next CEO."

A young manager named A.J. was there that day, and like the others, received a seed. He went home that evening and excitedly told his wife about the CEO's plan of succession.

"What does plant care have to do with running a company?" she asked.

"I asked myself that same question," he replied. "All I know is I think I'm ready for the presidency."

"You'd make a wonderful CEO. So let's not take this plant project lightly," she chorused.

The manager and his wife potted the plant, watered it and prayed over it. A.J. took gardening lessons at a local nursery and took his plant care seriously.

In three-to-four weeks, some of the other contestants reported how well their seeds were growing. A.J. kept checking his seed, but the sprout had not made it to the surface yet. Another two weeks passed. No sprout.

By now most of the others were talking about how well their plants were growing. Six months went by, but A.J.'s pot was still barren. He felt like a failure. He was confused. He knew he had done everything right. He didn't want to be embarrassed, so he didn't say anything to his friends or work associates.

A year finally went by and all of the other managers brought their plants into the conference room for inspection. A.J. apologized to his wife and then told her he was going to play golf instead of going to work that day. He felt sick to his stomach for having lost the opportunity to compete for the presidency.

"You promised your CEO that you'd show him what you could produce when you accepted that seed a year ago. I know the results are disappointing, but … "

"They're disastrous" he interrupted.

"Okay, they're disastrous then," she continued. "But you've got to keep your promise."

He took his empty pot, along with his thoroughly itemized check-list of plant care, to work. When he arrived, he was amazed at the variety of plants grown by his colleagues. They were beautiful and came in all shapes and sizes. When his colleagues saw his barren pot, some of them laughed at him. Others sympathized with him and offered him their condolences. Some were genuinely concerned and asked why he hadn't asked for their help during the year. Most sent the message by their words and by their actions that they were relieved he wasn't in the running.

When the CEO arrived, he surveyed the room and greeted the managers. A.J. sat in the back of the room behind one of the columns, trying his best to be invisible.

"My, what great plants, trees and flowers you have grown," the CEO said to the group of managers. "Today, one of you will be appointed my successor."

All of a sudden, the CEO spied A.J.'s pitiful pot.

"Whose pot is this?" he shouted.

A nervous chatter which escalated into giggles filled the room.

"Well?" the CEO replied.

"A.J.'s!" someone shouted.

"A.J.'s," another joined in.

"A.J., where are you, son?" the CEO asked.

When A.J. pried himself out from behind the column, a hush filled the room.

The CEO motioned for A.J. to come to the front of the room.

On his way up to the front, A.J. saw the CEO lean over to examine his documentation of plant care, including the nursery certificate.

The CEO smiled and shook his head before he spoke to the group of managers. He invited A.J. to step beside him and then put his arm around A.J.'s shoulders.

"I'd like to introduce you to your next CEO," the president announced.

A.J.'s eyes widened – but not as wide as everyone else's in the room.

"One year ago today, I gave each of you a seed. I told you to take the seed, plant it, and care for it. Forgive me for what I am about to say, but I gave all of you boiled seeds. A boiled seed will not grow. All of you brought me beautiful plants, trees, and flowers. But they are not from the seeds I gave you."

A collective gasp rose from all of the managers.

"When you found that your seeds wouldn't grow, you substituted another seed for the one I gave you. Everyone, that is, except A.J."

The CEO picked up A.J.'s checklist and showed it to the group.

"I'm holding a record of A.J.'s extraordinary accomplishments. It shows his dedication and discipline. It shows every ounce of his care. It is a testimony to his persistence – and honesty. He came here to face the music today. He was willing to accept the consequences of his efforts."

The CEO turned to A.J. and shook his hand.

"Congratulations, young man. Your training starts immediately. By the way, can you and your lovely wife join me for dinner tonight?"

A.J. accepted the invitation to the applause of his humbled and embarrassed, but much wiser colleagues.

(Adapted from the wisdom literature)

Have you ever extinguished your own flame of passion by trying to be something or someone other than your authentic self? Take a look in the mirror, and value the person looking back at you. Give yourself credit for your strengths, and celebrate your uniqueness. Be persistent in your honesty and values – and you will feel again the inner fire of passion and joy.

A Face at the Window

- Carol A. Hacker, M.S. -

*M*any years ago, I embarked on a somewhat thankless career as an employment counselor for the U.S. Department of Labor. I helped people on welfare find jobs. I also worked with drug addicts and alcoholics, as well as bums that were out to beat the system. I counseled ex-cons, child abusers, and molesters. There were times when I felt I only saw the seedy side of life. And then one day, something special happened.

It was a cold, damp, December morning. I turned on the lights in my office, got comfortable in my chair, glanced out the window, and started making plans for a new day. As 8 a.m. approached, I could hear co-workers talking about the weekend's activities as they arrived one by one. A few frisky birds chirped in the distance. Young children hurriedly passed outside of my office window, swinging their school bags, seemingly in anticipation of the week ahead.

The feeling that someone was watching me soon interrupted my thoughts. I glanced up and saw the sad face of a small, thin boy peering through the tinted, gray glass. When I smiled, he ran out of my sight. I thought about the child off and on throughout the day, as I had frequently seen him pass by, always alone, looking forlorn.

The rest of my day was filled with people, paperwork, and telephone calls. 3:30 brought early dusk with dark clouds and gentle snowflakes. The same lonely child appeared at my frosty window, only to whisper, "I love you" and disappear.

Through the years, I never forgot that day. Maybe it was because it was during a time in my life when I had hoped to start a family of my own, only to find out it was

183

not to be. Or, maybe that beautiful young face reminded me that there was more in the world than the tragedy I saw in the eyes of the adults I so desperately wanted to help.

Twenty-three years later on cold, winter days, I sometimes find myself looking out my office window and thinking about the child who appeared and disappeared out of my life in a day's time. He would now be more than 30 years old. Perhaps he is someone's husband; maybe he has children of his own. Hopefully, someone is the recipient of his sweet, "I love you."

Play Today!

**If you're too busy to play,
you're just too darn busy!**

Scott Friedman, CSP

The Cookie

- The Honorable Kristin H. Ruth -

I could smell the odor of wet diapers, formula and scrubbed floors as I entered the orphanage named Elisa Martinez, in Guatemala City. I listened for sounds of children, laughing, crying or talking in their native language. I heard nothing. I had been told there were probably 150 children under 5 years old who lived here. Was I in the right place?

The orphanage was difficult to find in the back streets of Guatemala City. When I drove up to the building, I didn't see any signs except a small numbered address by the discrete iron gate, near the entrance to the white stucco building. Other than a few plants surrounding the gate, the rest of the area was dry, dusty and barren. There was no fenced-in area, no playground, no toys or balls scattered around the plain white stucco building – nothing to indicate fun, happiness, exercise and laughter typically associated with a place that housed little children. I thought to myself: *Is this the place that so many abandoned children called their home?*

I entered the foyer area to find a vacant, worn out, brown wooden desk holding a couple of pens and pencils, a sign-in sheet and a black rotary dial telephone placed strategically on the left hand corner. A little silver bell ringer was on the right and I hit it twice without hesitation. To the left I could see a narrow hall that housed little offices, and to my right was another hall that would take me to a world I had never seen, but would soon never forget.

A lovely dark-haired, small-framed lady in a pink uniform dress came to the front to see who was ringing the bell.

I felt very much alone and asked her, in broken Spanish, if I could speak with the director. She asked me to wait; in a few minutes I was sitting in one of the small offices with a very distinguished lady who seemed a bit skeptical of why I was there.

A Guatemalan attorney I'd spoken with earlier knew of this orphanage, and had made the connection for me to visit. I was interested in the adoption process and wondered if any of these children were available. Apparently, the majority of the children who are dropped off at the orphanage are seldom declared legally abandoned and are therefore not eligible for adoption. Once dropped off at the orphanage, most of these children will never see a parent or relative again. The director tried to explain to me that it is difficult for the children to have visitors, as they all think and hope that they will be "the chosen one" taken home with someone, anyone. Their little hearts and minds are filled with hope as they never give up their dream of just going "home."

I convinced the director to escort me down the hall to the right. I could see several big rooms adjacent to smaller rooms holding a few tables, chairs, and a few toys. The 3- and 5-year-olds had to play in these rooms, since there was no outside playground. When I looked in the window of one of the little rooms, about 15 children ran to the door and started laughing, jumping up and down and yelling. As I entered the room I could not believe what I felt as each child ran up to me, stretching out their arms for me to pick them up and hold them. The little girls were dressed in colorful, clean dresses, obviously donated to the orphanage. They all looked so beautiful with their coal black hair, dark eyes and light brown complexions. Many had black patent leather shoes with a strap across the top of the foot; others wore tennis shoes. Most of the shoes didn't fit, but the children didn't seem to mind. They smiled, cheered, and called me "mama." Each wanted to take my hand, rub my face, hold my long hair, crawl up my leg or just touch me. Until they saw me, "the visitor," they had been quiet, just sitting or looking at a few toys and books. They were not used to the morning hugs, kisses and daily love and affection I have always taken for granted. Their mundane life was one of routine...eating, sleeping and waiting for someone to take them "home" and love them. Who could leave these beautiful children?

My research on adoption had opened my eyes to what a Third World country and its people endure every day. Seeing the desperation on the faces of pregnant women standing by a hot grill, selling their tortillas at the market place while an infant sits below, in a box wrapped in the colorful cloth that had been hand-woven during the middle of the night. The daily newspapers were filled with heart wrenching stories, such as women who left their babies in tin cans on the railroad tracks to be totally crushed and left unidentifiable, and begging children shot on the street because they are a menace to the tourists. In reality, a mother, who truly loves her baby, recognizes her desperate situation and leaves another beautiful child in the care of a place called Elisa Martinez. No questions asked.

Suddenly, I heard a loud clapping sound. All of the children scrambled toward what I called the "big room." They sat with their backs to the wall, so quietly I could have heard a pin drop. I wondered to myself what was going on, as the children were obviously accustomed to this event. Almost simultaneously, two women came out with trays of what looked like sugar cookies. The women made their way around the room and one by one, each child was given the treat of the day. They were happy, but silent.

Then, all of a sudden, a small toddler started to cry. He had not made his way to the wall and had been passed up by the woman with the cookies. I ran over to pick him up and comfort him. The director, seeing my expression, told me to leave the child alone – he would have to learn for himself what behavior was expected in order to get his afternoon cookie. My instinct was to continue to cuddle the small boy, but I realized I was interfering in the routine, since approximately 75 children were lined up against the wall, performing perfectly. If this little boy was going to survive, he would have to learn how the system worked.

As I turned away from the little boy, the tears welled up in my eyes. I could not imagine how important one sugar cookie could be in this little person's life. It was the highlight of his day.

It was getting late and my heart had endured more than I could have imagined, but I wanted to see the last room where little babies were lying in cribs. There were only about five women who worked here, with the responsibility of taking care of at least 150 children, 25 or so under the age of one. They were amazing, sweet women who did an incredible amount of work each day because they loved these children. I looked in the room and expected to hear crying and baby noises. Instead, I heard very little. Most of the babies have given up on crying, since there was no one to help them or pick them up when they cry. I looked into the cribs, and the most beautiful babies would peer up at me with their black hair sticking up, wrapped in cheese cloth diapers and little T-shirts of various colors. Most of them had only one little sheet or blanket. I noticed that many of them were lying on their stomachs with their bottoms in the air, rocking back and forth. My tears started flowing again as I realized they were rocking themselves, because no one else was there to do it for them. I thought of how precious and lonely these children were, and how they accommodated their own needs by the little motions of moving back and forth. How delicate, sweet and innocent each of these little people were. Imagine what the lack of the human touch and a mother's love will eventually cost them.

I reached down and picked up one little boy who was rocking so hard his bed was squeaking. After a few minutes of holding this little boy in my arms, he fell asleep. I could have held him forever. I asked the director if he had a name and she said, "Etomal." He had been left right after he was born, and they had received no word from anyone since. Etomal was one of the many children abandoned by their parents, but unless he is legally given up for adoption by his biological parents, he will wait it out at Elisa Martinez until he is moved to an orphanage which houses older children.

I have been back several times to visit Etomal, but lost track of him after he was moved to another orphanage. The last time I was there, when Etomal was about 3 years old, I walked into that familiar little room on the side of the big room. He was sitting there with his back to the door. When I said his name, he turned to me and said, "Mama." My heart stopped – I could not believe he remembered me – or maybe I was just another vision of hope for him to leave the orphanage. I stayed with  him as long as I could that day, but in my heart I knew this little boy would become another statistic on the street. In the three years he had been at Elisa Martinez, no one had come to visit him but me.

That was the last time I saw Etomal. We had a great time that day, as I brought many gifts and candy for Etomal and the other children. (You soon learn that if you bring for one, you must bring for all.) All I have now is a picture to remind me of my little friend.

My heart is forever changed from my visits to Guatemala and the orphanage. My memory of the little boy who rocked so hard that his crib squeaked will forever be in my mind and heart. Every day at 3:00 p.m., I remember "the cookie" and think about the many little children lined up against a wall waiting for the best part of their day.

I pause to count my many blessings. It is so easy to take all we have for granted, and allow the little things to depress and frustrate us. When that happens, remember what one little sugar cookie meant to the children at Elisa Martinez, and be thankful for the abundance in your life.

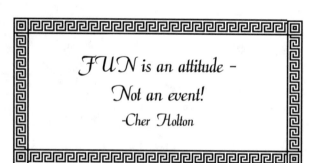

*FUN is an attitude –
Not an event!*
-Cher Holton

Against All Odds

- Alton Jamison -

Sometimes we can't stop the waves from crashing down;
Sometimes we can't control the way the wind blows;
Sometimes we can't control the pain that causes us to frown;
Sometimes things happen and the reason only God knows.

Failure and disappoint sometimes go hand and hand;
Every time I fail at something I become disappointed;
Often times I'm disappointed for my failure to understand;
Why in the world are things going this way, if I'm God's anointed?

When your eyes are filled with tears, and the tissues are running low;
When your body is drained and your spirit is
     too weak to regain control;
When agony of despair has overtaken you like a shadow;
When the worries of this life have anchored themselves
     in your soul –

That's when Against All Odds you must succeed;
That's when Against All Odds you must continue to press
     towards the mark;
That's when Against All Odds you mustn't quit.

That's when – Against All Odds ...

The Angina Monologues

- Mark Drury -

I was in the middle of a life transition when a bad experience happened to me on October 1, 2001. I suffered a heart attack and had a quadruple bypass heart procedure two days later. It was almost as much fun as having your wisdom teeth removed through your ears.

I had written the whole chest pain thing off as a torn muscle. I had been doing barbell squats about an hour before it happened. I was sure I had cracked a rib or something. I was swimming at the time the chest pains began, so I pulled my big old torso out of the pool. I went back to the locker room, showered, dried off, changed clothes, and decided to drive myself home. I figured I had hurt a rib.

On the way home, the pain convinced me to take a detour to the Suburban Hospital emergency room, parking in the handicapped spot. (When my brother removed my car from the lot the next day, he discovered a citation clipped under my windshield wiper for parking there. In my book, heart attack is right up there in the "handicapped" category.)

They gave me an EKG right away and determined my pain was definitely not a heart attack; however, they wanted to keep me for observation overnight. They drew blood. Eight hours later, they drew blood again. Another eight hours later, they drew blood yet again. That third blood test told the hard, cold truth. I had indeed suffered a heart attack. Cardiac enzymes do not lie. Bummer!

They immediately scheduled me for a cardiac catherization the next day. I was somewhat sedated as they drove a big old piece of garden hose up the vein in my right inner thigh. It can best be summed up as a very warm rush all over your body. I could see the monitors overhead as the team of cardiologists were studying this rush of liquid dye surging through my veins. It was like this juice was flowing through my veins and all of a sudden it hit a road block. I knew the news was not good because I could see all four cardiologists rubbing their chins, shaking their heads as if looking at a bad stock portfolio report, and murmuring, "tsk, tsk, tsk." My cardiologist must have been a traffic cop at one time because he had all kinds of expressway analogies. He told me, "Mark, it looks like there are stalled cars in the left lane on I-64, I-65, I-264, and I-71." He told me that I had major blockage in four main arteries. I replied, "What if I just stay off the interstates altogether and take the back roads?"

I was immediately put on the tarmac, scheduled to be the next plane to take off on Quadruple Bypass Airlines. I was given a two-hour window to get ready for surgery. I begged to postpone it until the next morning, and got a 16-hour reprieve. I needed time to get ready. I was one scared young man who needed someone to say something wonderful and comforting to soothe me. I was more upset that evening than at any time in my life. I think I literally cried from 9 p.m. that Tuesday night until 4 a.m. without stopping.

My story has a catchy, funny title, but this is serious stuff here. My personal crisis was this terrible surgery looming over my head, but it could be anything. We all have one time in our lives when we just cannot handle the news that came in the form of a letter, a medical report, a policeman at the door, a phone call in the night, or a memo in our employee mail slot. There will be that one time in your life when your knees buckle underneath you and your world collapses. How do you handle the next two hours, two days, two months, or two years?

I got the best piece of advice of my life from a wonderful young man who wandered in my room at 4 a.m. to get my vital signs. He was a 30-year-old registered nurse named Thomas. He was six feet tall, all smiles and teeth, strikingly handsome, and full of compassion. He could tell that I had been on a major crying jag and knew that I needed some major comforting.

"Any words of wisdom for someone like me, four hours before this ordeal that I am about to go through?" I asked.

"Mark," he said, "do you believe in God?"

"Yes, I do, although I am not a regular at church on Sunday."

> *There will be that one time in your life when your knees buckle underneath you and your world collapses. How do you handle the next two hours, two days, two months, or two years?*

Thomas continued. "Mark, there comes a time in every-one's life when you have to turn your life over to God, or a parent, or a wife, or your friends, just for a little while. There will be a time when you just can't function for yourself. I want you to pick a date, let's say one week from this Sunday. Right now, this morning at 4 a.m., put yourself in God's hands for the next 11 days and let Him take care of you. Worry about nothing, for you will not be able to take care of things yourself. Trust Him and the people He put on earth that know and love you to tend to you and your needs. I want you to wake up on Sunday morning, October 14th and resume your life as you knew it. That, my friend, is how you will get through this ordeal."

How that man got to be so wise at such a young age is simply beyond me. When he finished speaking to me, I cried no more. I placed myself and my care into God's hands that night and went into surgery with that mindset. I was still afraid, but not worried after that. He was right. I was unable to take care of my breathing, my hygiene, my mobility, my eating, my finances, my job, my transportation, my house, or anything else for a part or all of those 11 days. But I had the most wonderful support system in place. The best group of family, friends, work associates, medical helpers, and neighbors in the world. I was so loved. I knew it all along but it took a game of volleyball with my heart to make me realize the depth and width of this love. God had been watching over me the whole time and I was so unaware. I talk all the time about angels in my life. Thomas was most definitely an angel from God sent in at just the right time that night – just when I needed it most.

I woke up on the morning of October 14th and reclaimed my life. It just so happened to be my 46th birthday. I had set a goal to be well enough in mind and body to begin taking charge again. I was not ready to do any barbell squats and still could not drive, but make no mistake. I was in control and it felt good. I completed a 12-week cardiac rehab program at the hospital, was walking the treadmill on an incline at a breakneck speed, and was heaving those cast iron dumbbells six weeks after surgery. Less than six months after surgery, I was performing a barbell aerobics class on stage at the Louisville Fitness Expo. I wonder how many people who saw me on stage twice that weekend had any idea the cute guy up there doing barbell squats in time to the tune *Send Me an Angel* had indeed been sent an angel, and had just endured a horrific operation that past fall.

In the classic novel, *The Scarlet Letter*, the heroine, Hester Prynne, is forced to wear the red letter "A" on her chest to remind the townspeople that she was an adulteress. I have an 11-inch vertical scar on my chest from my surgery that is red and resembles the letter "I." I wear my letter "I" proudly to represent the fact that "I" survived, that "I" am loved, and that "I" am more appreciative of life and the world around me than I ever was before my ordeal.

Depending On the Kindness of Strangers

- Carol Spielvogel -

*H*ave you ever gotten what you had been asking for, and working for? Something that had taken a number of years to accomplish? It happened to me in August of 2001. I was so high I felt like the master of my own universe! Isn't it funny how when you get what you ask for, so much more comes with it?

My husband and I had just moved to Canada, a gigantic leap of faith for us, and a particular dream come true for me. I felt like I was home! Then came the surprise.

Before we had even gotten completely unpacked, I discovered a lump. Then I learned it was malignant. What a blow! Surely God had not brought me way up here, let me totally disrupt my life, just to die!

Suddenly I felt like a stranger in a strange land. I had an entirely new health care system to deal with that didn't know what to do with me because I was "from away." They didn't understand the rules of insurance companies and many other things. So not only did I have to deal with the cancer, surgery, chemotherapy and radiation, I had to deal with new systems, getting settled, and – oh yes – let's throw Christmas into the mix as well. Welcome to Canada!

But I learned something through it all that I could not have learned any other way. I was quickly humbled, realizing I actually had no control over anything! It totally threw me. After all, I had done everything right, yearly tests, etc. yet I had to come here to have something discovered that apparently had been there for several years!

One day during the period I was receiving chemotherapy, when I was feeling at my worst, the kindest thing happened to me. There was a knock on the door and a lady I had never seen before introduced herself and handed me a card. She said she had heard I was sick and just wanted me to know someone cared. I almost cried. In another couple of days, my real estate agent came to the door, bringing a lovely bouquet of flowers, along with goodies to eat. She just wanted me to know she was thinking of me and would be glad to help.

There was a lady who worked in the local hardware store whom I had only met a few times. She arrived one night with flowers, then returned to visit often. I was attending a local church and a woman I'd met there only once e-mailed me. She told me I seemed to be the independent type, probably finding it difficult to ask for help, but having been in a similar situation, she assured me I was going to need help. She became my e-mail prayer partner. The church pastor was also a great source of encouragement, always showing up at the exact right time. Everywhere I turned, people were so kind to me – and they didn't even know me! I was totally amazed at all this. Here I was, far away from my usual support system, yet these new angels came to form a new, local branch in my support system. Each one of these strangers gave me support and encouragement whenever I needed.

Some months later, when I was feeling much better, I was walking along the shore looking at the calm waters. The thought that came to mind was the bible verse: *He leadeth me beside the still waters, He restoreth my soul* (Psalm 23: 2-3). At that very moment a seal popped up his head and stared me right in the eyes. This tremendous feeling of peace and well being came over me and I knew I was in my right place.

I am fine now but in this one year my priorities have really undergone a restoration. I learned quickly what is important to me in life. I also learned that you are never alone. I always heard that your needs are met at the point of the need – and this was living proof to me. The sicker I got the more people appeared. There are no guarantees in life but one: you will always be taken care of, especially when you need it most.

(Artwork by Bil Holton. Ph.D.)

The Marks We Leave

- Mark Sanborn, CSP, CPAE -

As time goes on and we reflect
On the things we've said and done;
The places we've been, the people we've met
And we think of all the fun.

We realize the marks we leave in life
Aren't made of stone or steel
But rather of the lives we've touched
 And how we make folks feel.

For people are far more valuable
Than achievements great and high,
Than cars or planes or space shuttles
Or buildings reaching to the sky.

You and I can leave our mark in life
By doing all we can
To serve and praise and uplift
The lives of children, women and men.

Lessons in Leadership:
The Power of Edification
- Vrsula C. Mannix -
Certified MasterStream Instructor

*O*ne of the most powerful rekindling tools in business today is EDIFICATION – a common concept that remains almost unheard of in traditionally-structured organizations. The result is that countless opportunities to enhance relationships and build business are lost every day. Bottom line – if your staff doesn't know how to edify you and your organization properly, they're compromising your credibility and weakening relationships with your prospective and existing customers – as well as the media, your vendors, the business community, your shareholders and anyone else with whom you seek a beneficial relationship.

Edification is simply a way of giving credibility to your company and the individuals engaging in the business relationship. It is a process through which each party comes to regard the others with greater respect – and themselves with greater pride. Done properly, edification establishes the individuals and the organizations they represent as being credible, significant and valuable to one another.

What makes edification more powerful than typical methods for enhancing credibility? The answer is in three parts: WHAT is said, WHO is saying it, and WHEN it is being said.

In fact, proper edification is one of the most effective tools for managing a prospect's level of productive tension. Let's take a closer look:

WHAT Is Said

Proper edification involves sharing two types of information: Factoids & Humanizers.

Factoids are the important pieces of information your prospect should know about the person with whom they are talking. It includes names, titles, responsibilities, company represented, quantifiable accomplishments and so forth.

Humanizers are interesting and relevant bits of personal information that help to showcase the nature – the human side – of the individual being edified. Here is an example:

Let's say that you have decided to go on a few sales calls with each of your representatives. Obviously, your purpose in going is to enhance your company's relationship with its prospects – and as a result, secure their business.

If your representatives behave like typical sales representatives, they will tell their prospects, "My manager and I would like to stop by for a few minutes Tuesday afternoon. What time would be best for you?" What's the problem? Being identified as a non-specific "manager" does nothing to enhance your image or boost the importance of your visit. In fact, it can actually make the sales representatives appear ineffective in executing their job.

On the other hand, if your sales representatives had said "I'm very fortunate to have Richard Reynolds spending time with me next Tuesday. Mr. Reynolds is one of our company's top managers and a huge resource for helping me help my clients. I only have him for the afternoon and he's asked me to set up just a few appointments with key people." This statement positions you in a much more favorable light – and increases the prospect's level of productive tension. As a result, the prospect is more likely to be receptive to the visit … the visitors … and the reason they're visiting.

The goal is to help your prospects realize that *they* are important because *important* people are electing to meet or speak with *them*.

WHO Should Say It

If you haven't already figured it out, *you* should never edify *yourself*. The core of what gives edification its power is that it is done by someone else on your behalf. If you were to edify yourself, you would come across as arrogant – turning your prospects off at the precise time you want to build rapport and trust. Expect a cold reception now and a closed door in the future if you try this route! If, however, someone else edifies you, you appear important and gracious – and your prospects will open up and provide the information you need to help support your business relationship – and ultimately secure more business.

When you arrive at your appointment, the representative should first introduce the prospect to you and *edify* the *prospect*. Then, the representative should introduce you to the prospect and *edify you*.

The dialog would go something like this: "Mr. Reynolds, allow me to introduce Sharon Skyler. Ms. Skyler is the Director of International Operations and she has been sharing with me some of the challenges they're facing where we might be of help."

"Ms. Skyler, this is Richard Reynolds, our Regional Director of Sales. He has been with our company for over 20 years – and has been instrumental in helping me develop solutions for my clients. I wanted the two of you to have a chance to meet."

Once the representative has made these introductions and properly edified the individuals, *you* greet the prospect and *edify* the *representative*.

"Ms. Skyler, it's a pleasure to meet you. I'm so glad you're working with Jim. He's been with us for six years now and is one of our most respected representatives – and he's shared some very impressive things with me about you and your company."

WHEN It Is Said

As you can see, the edification process generally takes place when introductions are made of the individuals involved in a business interaction. Delaying it further would put everyone in an awkward position, which would actually *raise* relationship tension instead of *reduce* it – and that's the opposite of what you are attempting to do.

While it may seem that edification could be performed prior to the start of the solutions presentation, to do so will most surely damage the sale for at least three reasons:

1. To delay edification that long into the process would mean that since you arrived, you've been sitting there as some mysterious stranger unwittingly raising tension the whole while.

2. The longer your presentation is, the lower your prospect's tension sinks – so edifying would lower tension further than desired at this time.

3. Most importantly, your prospect didn't really agree to get together to hear about *you* or your company anyway – they just want to solve *their* problem – so introduce and edify everyone at the beginning and then get on with business.

Remember that initiating, building and maintaining mutually-beneficial business relationships is an important part of *many* of your employee's jobs throughout your organization – and that means they should *all* understand the importance of proper edification.

Edify everyone at the outset of any discussion, and you're setting the stage for success!

An Attitude of Gratitude

- Debra Atkinson -

*I*t's been a year, maybe two, of ups and downs: the stock market, the economy, your investment statements, our nation's patriotism.

Have you been able to find the blessings there? Thankfulness for having had something to lose at all? Thankful you lost it, yet you're still "OK?"

Are you able to be thankful if your health was taken from you, the rug pulled out from under your feet, that you have options, choices, medicine and maybe some *time* to take advantage of while you're here?

Are you thankful for those around you who are suffering from illness, yet who are enlightening you? Are they not, ironically, the very ones who point out the blessings we each have, who bring life back to its simplest terms, and humble us by their good faith? They have the ability to see the glass half full vs. half empty. Let me share an example:

A 44-year-old man, married with two children, thrived on an active lifestyle until three years ago. He enjoyed sailing, skydiving, traveling, softball, and heavy involvement in his children's and his church's activities. Three years ago he was diagnosed with Still's Disease and he's since baffled Mayo Clinic. (Now that may have earned him a degree of status among the good doctors up North, but it's a status he'd gladly trade.)

His voice and facial features have been barely recognizable to family and friends at times due to the Prednisone use. He and his wife praise the drug's ability to spare him from the pain and other symptoms of the disease.

While his fatigue kept him and his family from attending many extra-curricular activities, they gave thanks for the quiet times together playing games, knowing this shared time would be remembered as a blessing.

He and his wife have beaten a path to Rochester from their home, putting many miles on their vehicle over these years. They continually give thanks for God's wisdom in their geographic proximity to the best medical care, and a retired set of grandparents who are always ready to step in when needed.

When a mass grew in his throat to the point he couldn't swallow, and it grew back not twice, but three times, they gave thanks for the quick medical care that led to an emergency tracheotomy.

Months turned to years of Prednisone use, weakening this man's bones to the point that a cough in the summer of 2001 caused a bone fracture in his spine. This led to the discovery that his spine was literally disintegrating in places. It meant surgery to place a steel plate in his spine to support his back, which in turn led to months of recovery and rehabilitation away from his family. But thankfully, they reminded us, they caught it early and there are treatments to improve the status of his bone integrity.

As 18 months of feeding tube use slowly came to an end and this man has literally learned to swallow again, he gave thanks for the option of using anesthesia when they removed the tube. After 18 months of liquid meals, what's another two hours under anesthesia, right? Well, no. "Get it out now," he told them.

He nearly cried over a bowl of soup at a bakery on the way home. Now, you all may have tears of joy when a new Panera Bread opens, but it won't be quite as moving an experience perhaps!

The ability to open e-mail and get a new update has been both a blessing and a curse. At times the keyboard has been damp with tears of celebration over a triumph like walking around the block, at times it's been tears of frustration over a setback. But knowing the situation was still better than wondering. In no other way could his family have reached so many of us directly; the list of names has grown to nearly a full page. And each of us in turn shares with so many others. That's a lot of 'net prayers.' Can't hurt.

There are times when you ask "why?" Even "why me?" or "why not me?" But through the roller coaster ride, the constant message of this patient family has been faith, trust, and thanks for all the blessings that are there – if you look.

Are you looking?

This Thanksgiving, I'll be able to sit across the table from this man at dinner, instead of having him in the living room with a feeding tube and his liquid lunch. I'll be thankful for this brother of mine, his family, and his amazing strength and faith.

This year I'll gladly give that man my slice of pumpkin pie and not argue about whose is bigger. My mother may faint. Maybe, just maybe, I'll give him my Cool Whip, too. They'll have to carry her away in a stretcher.

The Lights in the Midst of the Tunnel

- Diana Hershberger -

About seven years ago, I was diagnosed with a disease that has kept me in large part in a dark, lonely tunnel. You see, I have Bipolar Disorder (manic depression). When in the deep recesses of the tunnel, my whole body feels weighted down, air feels stagnant and the oxygen is low. After years of struggling with this illness, I have come to learn there may not be a light at the end of the tunnel, because the illness cannot be cured. However, it can be managed, and I hold onto hope with each light that illumines the tunnel in intermittent valleys. I have come to tell myself to go with what I know, not what I feel. To go strictly on what I feel would bring the tunnel crashing down around me, snuffing out any existing light.

Manic depression affects 1 percent of the U.S. population and this is probably a conservative count, since 75 percent of those with Bipolar Disorder go undiagnosed. Large leaps have been made with medication, but there is no actual cure. My disease manifests itself in several ways. I am what is referred to as a rapid-cycler. I'll be feeling fine, even giddy (manic) or extraordinarily irritated, then within minutes come down and feel depressed, sad, alone – crying, sleeping. It's taken me years and six psychiatrists to find a medication combination which gives me more access to the lights in my dark tunnel. Although I don't stay "stable" for long, my medications have afforded me some respites in the challenges I face with this illness. I try to hold on to these when I am at my darkest times.

I am very fortunate. I have a Lord I know loves me and holds my hand when the tunnel is at its darkest. I also have several family and friend support systems that, though they can't understand my illness, recognize it and stay "closer than a brother." It was a close friend who recognized my symptoms and encouraged me to get help.

I am writing this to encourage you not to give up. If you struggle with or know someone who struggles with Bipolar Disorder – or any other chronic illness – please don't give up. Though there may not be a light at the end of the tunnel or cure, there will be lights in the midst of the tunnel. You will experience them when you find an even balance of health professionals, the right combination of medication, and a strong support network. Reach out to those who love you. They just may want to help. There is no cure, but there is hope. Look for the joy in every "light" experience. Embrace the lights in the midst of the tunnel.

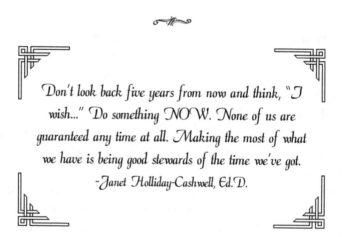

Don't look back five years from now and think, "I wish..." Do something NOW. None of us are guaranteed any time at all. Making the most of what we have is being good stewards of the time we've got.

-Janet Holliday-Cashwell, Ed.D.

One Moment in Time

- Edie Raether, M.S., CSP -

*The time is November, 1988. The event is the
Wisconsin Women's State Volleyball Tournament.
The teams are Shawano v. Kaukauna.*

⌐╫⌐

*T*he pressure was on! Since Shawano had taken
second in the state's volleyball tournament in the
previous year ('87), the only way they could do better in '88
was to take first. The team knew no defeat, boasting a 41-0
winning season. With deafening cheers from fans wearing
red on one side and orange on the other, Round I of the
three-game series ended in disappointment for Shawano,
falling short by two points for a 14-16 loss. Stunned and
numb from their defeat, round II was off to a bad start, trail-
ing 0-5, when Shawano's invincible team called a time out
with hopes of regrouping. They had practiced various trig-
gers to create focus and release their *PowerZone* prior to the
tournament, but their anxiety seemed to be blocking their
mind-empowering strategies. They had also rehearsed ways
to get into the "flow" by making a conscious decision to
have fun and be playful, rather than allowing tensions to
interrupt their state of unconscious competence.

Their fears of defeat seemed to be determining their
self-imposed destiny, with the score now 0-13. Coach Matty
Mathison, who had also won the state's very first championship in 1973, had a tough decision to make: Do we
concede the game and allow those eagerly waiting on the
bench a few minutes in the big arena – or – do we believe
in miracles and go for the gold, even though we are two

points away from defeat and scoring even one point appears to be an impossibility?

Knowing the power of positive reinforcement, Coach Mathison took time to acknowledge and console her super-stars, saying "I'm so proud of you. We can feel great about taking the silver back to Shawano." In the silence that followed, a soft but determined voice was heard. It came from a more reserved player – one not normally looked to for leadership. Her words, which ignited instant inspiration, were simply, "We are going to win this game."

Whether it was the determination in the voice or the words she uttered, everyone listened and all obeyed. Even the coach decided to give the magic of miracles a chance, sending her team onto a floor flooded with predators who were already chanting their victory cries.

The Shawano team, in quiet confidence, gallantly returned to a most intimidating environment, ready to personify a course in miracles. The opposing team took position to serve the ball, preparing to claim their shut-out victory. To everyone's surprise, they served the ball into the net, giving hope to the pointless, but "never-say-die" Shawano girls, who proceeded to break their dismal spell by scoring six consecutive points. Intercepting the next serve of their somewhat shaken opponent, the Shawano girls went on to score 15 consecutive points, taking the game. With the rekindling of their human spirit, they went on to win the third game by a score of 15-3, thus becoming the 1988 Wisconsin State Women's Volleyball Champions.

Interestingly, it was at the 1988 Olympics that Whitney Houston released, "One Moment in Time." The Shawano Women's Volleyball Team had just experienced their "One Moment in Time!"

Fast forward to 1997. Coach Mathison relates another experience – her own personal "one moment in time." The coach who had inspired several teams to state championships in Division I was going through her own "dark night of the soul." She had lost all hope and her will to live. Things were crashing in around her, and she confesses to feelings of serious depression and despair. Later that year, as she was completing some paperwork, she inadvertently filled out forms to apply for *Disney's American Teacher of the Year Award.* Unbelievingly, she won for her division of health, physical education and wellness. It was like a message from the universe, revitalizing her spirit and her soul.

I think we all have those special moments when we feel despair and hopelessness. From some unlikely source, perhaps even our own inner voice, we receive a message of inspiration that stirs the soul and screams, "BASH ON!" Listen to your inner voice, and allow yourself to be rekindled!

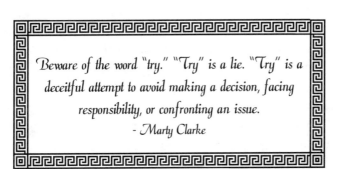

Beware of the word "try." "Try" is a lie. "Try" is a deceitful attempt to avoid making a decision, facing responsibility, or confronting an issue.
- Marty Clarke

Our Own 'Special Memory'

- Joyce Harris -

As we sat watching our children and grandchildren open their Christmas gifts, we saw the crumbled paper and crushed bows and wondered: Will anyone remember where these gifts come from? Will they even be able to find them later?

Some time passed, and after a family gathering, we discussed how we would like to give the children and grandchildren a special gift – one they would always remember; one that would not be crumpled, crushed, forgotten, lost, or thrown away, as so often happens with a well-intended gift. We have been blessed with 13 grandchildren. Shopping for gifts had always been a joy, but with the number of family members increasing, shopping had become quite time-consuming, as well as costly

We have always enjoyed the holiday gatherings, as well as other family time with our children and grandchildren – the sounds of laughter, crying, squeals of delights, cries of terror, hugs and kisses, joking, the aroma of cooking and baking, pictures being taken, doors slamming, diapers being changed, tears being wiped, grandchildren being held, sons and daughters talking with Mom and Dad, stories being read, and good night kisses for Grand Ma and Grand Bob. After much thought and discussion, we had a wonderful idea – why not create our own Special Memory? We would need something the children and grandchildren would not crumple, crush, forget, lose, throw away, or even outgrow! It would be a memory that all ages would enjoy, as ages ranged from 1 to 39.

Planning began for a special memory trip to Walt Disney World, a place for children of all ages, a magical place where special memories are made and shared. Calls were made and vacations were scheduled. The grandchildren were not to be told until the appointed time. On Christmas Eve each grandchild and parent gathered around the tree to receive their Mickey Mouse and Minnie Mouse ears. Of course Grand Ma and Grand Bob had to wear the famous Mickey and Minnie ears, too!

Each grandchild and parent was given a Mickey and Minnie gift bag which included an itinerary for our one-week, all-expenses-paid trip to Walt Disney World in Orlando, Florida for the week of February 16-22, 2002. Also included were the housing accommodations for all 23 family members. The pictures showed the many amenities, such as the heated swimming pool and game rooms we would all enjoy.

As the grandchildren pulled the items out of their gift bags, they squealed with delight. They cheered as they unpacked the Disney back packs to hold their souvenirs; the autograph books to gather their favorite Disney character's signatures. As they jumped around, the sound of merriment and joy could be heard in the anticipation of seeing Mickey Minnie, Winnie, and Cinderella.

We hired a photographer from Walt Disney World to take family pictures at Cinderella's castle. We told the parents the only payment we requested was to have the children and themselves ready for picture-taking on that one appointed day.

The next Christmas, as we watched our children and grandchildren open our special Christmas gift – the family picture taken in front of the castle at Walt Disney World – they all squealed with excitement! The gift card read:
We Created Our Own Special Memory!
>*Love, Grand Ma and Grand Bob*
>*Mom and Dad*

The Trees You Pass in the Forest

- Luba Havraniak -

*A*n old lady once told me something a long, long time ago. I often reflect back on her words, especially when I am disappointed in those people I love. As I grow older, I realize the significance of her words and how true they really are.

"People are nothing but the trees you pass in the forest of life. Do not base your personal happiness on them. They are subject to weather like trees in the wind, and are not as stable as they appear. As a tree's branch may break, so too are the people in your life. It is important to remember that they, like you, are fragile and can weaken or break easily. They are not permanent fixtures. Some will drift in for only awhile, others may stick around for some time. It is not fair to expect that your happiness comes from them, and it is not fair for them to make you responsible for theirs.

"The only way to attain happiness is through yourself. Therefore, you are responsible for it. You cannot blame others if they do not give you the happiness you need. They cannot be held accountable for all your wishes, desires, expectations, opportunities, loves, wants, needs and accomplishments. Only you can achieve them. We are all God's creatures. Accept people as they are, but most importantly, accept yourself. Be accountable for all the things you want in life.

"When you are in control of your feelings of happiness, you control your destiny. You will enjoy life much more when you take ownership of your feelings. Your rewards in life will be yours to enjoy, and nobody – and I mean nobody – can take that away from you. And nobody can shatter your happiness, but you."

To this day, I let no one interfere with my happiness. If someone disappoints me or makes me sad, I change my attitude. I am in control of my feelings, and he/she cannot make me sad. I enjoy my life now because I am responsible for my feelings. Whenever I reflect on that chance encounter with the old woman, I smile. She improved my life with her words. Now I want to share those same words with you, so that you too, can enjoy your life to the fullest.

(Artwork by Bil Holton, Ph.D.)

On-the-Job Training for the Role of a Lifetime

- Dana C. Foster -

*T*hroughout the world there must be thousands of different types of jobs people work hard preparing, applying, and competing for. However, once we are hired, a large majority of us over time begin to hate our jobs and often complain about the work requirements, coworkers, or the company's management (the boss and the rest of the higher paid crew).

Unfortunately, most stay with the company because of the good benefits, fear of change, or the uncertainty of being able to find another position that would pay as well. Perhaps others are upset with their jobs because they turn out to be nothing like they perceived them to be. Either they are boring or too challenging, overwhelming or unfulfilling, far to hectic or heading nowhere fast.

Conversely, there are many people who find just the opposite in their jobs, and love nearly every aspect. Maybe it just depends on how we decide to look at things. In my previous career, I too complained about my job – many, many times. However, at the end of the day I felt very fortunate and blessed, just having a source of income to provide for my family. In my humble opinion, the end truly justified the means.

Providing for our families is a responsibility that the bulk of us take very seriously. After all, the family should be ranked ahead of any place of employment, and I feel that being a parent is the most important role we could ever hope to play in our society, because it truly has one of the greatest impacts on it.

However, the total amount of preparation, skills, and training necessary to perform well in this role cannot be found in any school curriculum. Therefore, when I learned I was going to be a father, I really didn't have a clue as to what to really expect, nor what would really be expected of me. The only thing I knew for sure was that I was very excited about the fact I was going to be a father, and even more excited knowing this was my big chance to instill into someone what it takes to survive in this world.

I had big plans on teaching him all about the things I'd learned over my many years in life, and how to maneuver through all the problems, setbacks, and drama, so he could go straight ahead into happiness right away. However, before any of this came about, it was I who would become the student to this new person who just arrived in my life.

During my son's first year in life, I learned seven major lessons that have changed my life forever. No other person in my life could have mentioned, taught, or effectively prepared me for the on-the-job training I was about to receive.

Control

The very first lesson – Control – was one of the hardest to accept. You see, I didn't realize that when you become a parent, your life is never just your own ever again. No longer could I just jump in the car, put the top down, cruise to wherever, then come back whenever I wanted. I was now faced with responsibility, and my normal procrastination in planning was no longer a viable option.

Soon, my son had me working on a tight schedule of walking, feeding, changing, and cleaning. Although it took a good bit of time, and an ego adjustment, I finally surrendered to the fact that I was no longer a sole proprietor of my own personal time.

Patience

The second lesson learned – Patience – was almost as difficult as the first. My desire to pour all this information into my son's brain had to wait for his mind to develop over a period of time. Also, I had to acquire patience to wait for each stage of his development to happen, as well as learn to be untiring as I helped him improve his skills.

Love

Next was the lesson about Love. I didn't know I could go from being so self-absorbed to being a person who would give his life to protect someone without a moment's thought. I also learned that the love a child gives to you is one of the most blessed experiences a person could ever experience. After a long day at work, seeing your child's face light up when you walk in the house really makes it all worth while.

Guidance

Guidance was another challenging lesson for me. I found out that you can really only hope to help influence a child's actions, you can never completely control them, for they are born with free will. Most often, my son would not listen to me, but would watch everything that I would do and try to copy it. This meant that my big plans on lecturing him through life had to change a bit. Some of my lazy ways had to disappear, as well as some open anger. Today our communication channels are clear, positive, and productive.

Faith

Then came the lesson of Faith. After constant worry about his growth, protection, and future, over time I learned to replace worry with faith. Faith in my son, myself, and, of course, the Lord, that things will be fine if you just let them.

Worry never made one thing any better, but I know that my faith has and continues to do so.

Joy

From day one, I was learning more about the lesson of joy, but didn't really know it. However, each day the joy grew – from his first smile, to his first steps and beyond. My wife told me once we could all find joy in the face of a child as he or she discovered all the beautiful, natural things this world has to offer ... which brings me to my final lesson.

Relationships

As a person and a mother, my wife is a remarkable woman whom I truly love. But what she sacrificed in terms of emotions, pain, and suffering to bring this person into the world is incredible. Doing what she did – out of her love for me and my son – is one debt I'm not sure I could ever repay.

We hope to teach our sons (we now have three) how important relationships are, and that the keys to positive relationships involve both time and work. Together my wife and I will proceed with doing our level best as parents, so when our sons step out into the world on their own, they can become good citizens, making positive impacts in the world.

As the years go by, we both look forward to the job at hand and hopefully, to our eventual promotion to the role of grandparents. Yet another on-the-job experience!

Each Day

- Diane L. Merriett -

*E*ach day, on my walk home from the office, I am reminded of a valuable "life lesson" that is triggered simply by glancing at an unusual tree. The tree is not of a type thought rare or foreign, but it's more the tree's shape that accounts for this labeling – especially its roots.

Often, preoccupied rehashing the current land mine of office politics, or the latest family crisis, or the most recent obstacle to a dream life envisioned years ago, I have passed this tree many times without so much as a look up, always paying for my negligence with a stumble. That's because along this section of sidewalk, the tree's roots, so large and expansive, have lifted the path at least 4-5 inches from the ground. The roots have not only grown deep, but wide and sturdy above ground as well, giving the appearance of a wooden rope that doubly fastens the trunk to the earth beneath it.

Not long ago, in the nastiest of weather, I was forced to slow down while engaging this stretch of sidewalk, fearing that a misplaced step under such icy conditions could lead to something far more serious than a stumble. For some unknown reason, with each deliberate step taken in my approach, the tree, its trunk and its roots soon became my focal point. Strong winds fiercely whipped the branches of every other tree on the block, but not this one. Some trees bent, and some trees swayed, but not this one. It was not the affect of the weather's rage on the tree that became the point of interest, but the lack of it. So I slowed my pace even further, finally stopping completely, taking it all in.

Then I got it. The tree had made its message known. Once it too, had been young and defenseless against the elements, but its roots held on. For a while, in its growth, it too, had bent against some stormy winds, yet its trunk sustained it. Time after time, the environment had created conditions that might have confined and restricted its growth, yet its roots grew deep and wide. And now, here it stood, anchored and unfazed in the face of a roaring wind, because with each storm it had previously endured, it had grown taller and stronger.

After a few moments, I felt a smile forming in the corner of my mouth. With a thumbs-up salute to the tree, I resumed my walk home, amazed by the silent encouragement of its simple existence, and thankful for a new way of looking at the storms of life that come our way each day.

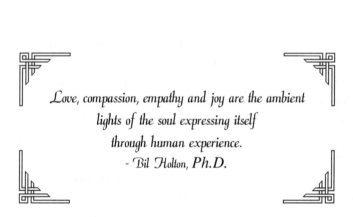

Love, compassion, empathy and joy are the ambient lights of the soul expressing itself through human experience.
- *Bil Holton,* *Ph.D.*

Love's Sunrise

- Audrey Williams -

One day close to sunset, I met a man in Charleston, South Carolina. He was a fine looking gentleman with a clean shave and a way about him that was sure and confident. He was impressive and bold, with flair and a conservative style. He was whimsical and playful, yet focused and reserved. He had an ambitious drive that was unprecedented – a smile that was warm and sincere.

He was curious and coquettish. He knew where he was going. He had already been places and done things and met important people, yet he held an ancestral exuberance. He seemed to cradle his familial roots as though their ethnicity would slip away. He acknowledged and respected their depth. He boasted that he was "the grandson of a sharecropper!"

He was determined to show the world and me that he was unique. And he was. He was admirable, resolute and rare. He was impressive, as a gentle giant. He had much to offer, and was ready to meet any challenge life presented with the intelligence and perspective of a much older man. Yet, he was youthful and vigorous. He lacked little, it seemed.

So, I wondered on that humid Sunday evening in July as we parted ways, if he would ever again grace me with the aura of his presence. And he did. He became consistent and persistent. He had seen something he admired and desired. So, he effortlessly surprised me, humored me, intrigued and angered me all in one sweep. He knew what he was doing. I did too.

He wanted to lead, but I could not follow. So, I quietly hoped and prayed that he might one day light a path to make the journey easier. He could have. The goodness and the power were within him. He had no fear except a brazen one that reached into the hereafter; one he knew could be overcome via a simple choice. He seemed invincible and above reproach, so he left me no choice.

I chose to observe him from afar. It was much easier on the heart. As days and weeks passed, through my inner spirit I could see him more clearly. My subconscious would not allow me to embrace trust in this enigma of a man. I was stirred by him, but not shaken. I could see him in my mind, yet he was not there. He was as a painter's canvas. I finally put the paintbrush away. It was a masterpiece that would never be completed. It would have been a magnificent one, but I had the power to roll the canvas away.

As I eased back and reflected on that bookstore greeting in the south, I was brought to a very special place. I had been there before. It was all too familiar. It was a place not everyone gets to visit. I released a half-smile because it was still one of my favorite places. A place I affectionately called *Love's Sunrise*.

"I've learned that as long as there's a sunrise, there's always hope for a majestic sunset!"

Little Angels

- Tammy Summers -

*C*hildren … laughing, adventurous, curious, innocent, loving, accepting, risk-taking, trusting, pure
and holy … Sometimes I feel that I have kissed the face of
God when I touch and kiss a child. I often sense that I am
on holy ground. It is overwhelming at times. Sometimes I
just watch and listen as I observe kids at play. I smile and
breathe deeply. Their tenderness amazes me. Their passion
for life inspires me, energizes me and calls me forth to
deeper, more honest living. Children remind me that there is
hope for our world after all.

I love children with my whole heart. So why have I
chosen not to have kids of my own? This is a question many
have asked me over the years, as they watched me interact
with children, at times slowly slipping into another place
and time with them. I can so easily become "one of them!"
Those times remind me of my freedom and innocence,
bringing me to a place when all in the world seems "right."
My eyes and heart open once again to the wonder and mystery of God.

So, why *have* I chosen not to have kids of my own? I
have asked myself this question many times. The nurturing
spirit was certainly there, but the passion and the *calling*
was just not in my heart. It took me a long time to get total
clarity on this issue, partially because I adore children and
don't want to "miss out" on anything fun in life! There was
also the cultural pressure of being raised as a "southern
woman." I mean, what nurturing "woman of character" does
not *want* to have children? What Christian woman in the
Bible belt doesn't feel like being a "mom" is, or should be,
their primary calling and their source of completion in life?

Now, that is pressure! Yet, in straining to listen to my heart, the answer slowly became clear. My calling was not to be a mother to my own children. As a dear friend of mine said years ago, "Tammy, I think you are going to have hundreds of children you will nurture along the way, but I don't see you having your own." Her words resonated deep within my soul. Prophetic.

What does all of this have to do with "Rekindling the Human Spirit?" I have experienced a unique place of giving and receiving incredible strength, love, nurturance, and yes, a *rekindling* of mutual spirits through my relationships with kids. As I mentioned earlier, children touch my soul in ways that that no adult can. They bring life, joy, zest, passion, laughter and enthusiasm to the core of my being. They energize me to go out and love in fuller, deeper, more unconditional ways. Indeed, they call me to a higher place – a more soulful living.

So how could I possibly "rekindle" the little spirit of a child? How could I possibly return what they have given to me? I believe that a woman without children of her own potentially has a special and sacred role in the lives of children. A woman available in this way can give one of the most precious gifts of all to a child – the gift of TIME and PRESENCE.

A mother often needs a break! She is responsible for her children 24/7 and often has several bambinos running around, distracting and irritating her with all that comes with being a full-time mom.

When I am with my nephews, nieces, and godchildren; the inner-city children I mentor; or any other children whose lives have graced mine, I have one primary focus – THEM. My goal is to listen, affirm, love, and adore them with all that I have. I am not distracted by laundry, meals, disciplining, fighting or their dad! I want to make them feel as valued and special as I can in those few hours or days I have with them. I want them to leave knowing how loved and important they are and that someone else in this world (besides mom and dad!) is CRAZY about them and is their biggest cheerleader!

My role is a *supplement* to the hard, daily work of parenting. It is a "coming along side of," mentoring, mothering, nurturing role that by its very definition allows me to be *totally present* in ways that a parent sometimes can't. What an incredible gift and encouragement to us all. To me, this unique relationship with children is one of the noblest ways I choose to rekindle my spirit and in the process, rekindle theirs. For this I am eternally grateful.

May you achieve the level of success you

EARN.

- *Bud Coggins*

Soars On the Wind

- Carla Royal, M.Ed. -

("B'darly Spring" is a nickname given to me by a dear friend. She affectionately dubbed me "B'darly" many years ago. After a crisis in my life, she added "Spring" to signify springing forth new life after a long winter.)

The wind supports me.
  The water supports me.
  The sand and rock and earth
      beneath my feet support me.
  The universe is calling me to life.
  Listen …
  Listen to the wind daring me to life.
  Listen to the water singing to me,
      teasing me to embrace life.
  Feel the ground beneath me
      supporting me, solid, sure, not giving way,
      demanding that I step fully into life.
  Watch the animals …
      they know nothing but living fully,
      even in the face of pain, fear, loss …
  They may feel fear, but they never question
      their worth, their validity, their right to be.
  I intend to be!
  I intend to be and to fully be!

And all the hawks came and soared above me.
  And I looked up and cried.
  They floated above me … for me.
  They said,
      "Fly, B'darly Spring, fly!"
  I looked up and said,
      "It hurts. It hurts!"
  And they said,
      "Of course it hurts.
      It hurts because you are not meant to be
      standing, looking up.
      You are meant to soar!"
  And I knew it to be true.

So true, that all I could do was lie down
    and cry, and weep, and laugh!
And all the leaves clapped and clapped
    … and still they clap.
And one by one the hawks lazily fly by me
    … teasing me.
I try to capture them with my camera but I can't.
They laugh and say,
    "We can't be captured, we are free!
    Fly, B'darly Spring … "
And I weep and I laugh …
    I don't know which it is.
And I know the universe fully supports me.
    And it cheers for me!
And just as quickly, I'm startled by
    a caterpillar that is fully being a caterpillar …
    crawling as it must, unselfconsciously, unknowingly
        … on me!

And in the midst of the tears of sadness and joy
I feel the fear of my own painful self-consciousness.
    Might someone come upon me in such a state?
    Would they think me crazy?
    I don't care! I do care! I don't want to care!
This is as real as anything I've ever felt!
And the sadness feels good when it is not stuck inside.
The tears are warm and comforting.
They don't frighten me. They are welcome.
And the leaves clap louder.
And the wind dares me to be free, to soar.
The wind laughs with me.
The wind has laughed all day.
    Open your wings, B'darly Spring, and soar.
And the wind dries my tears as fast as I can cry them,
    turning them into joy.
I struggle to stay in the moment. My mind rushes ahead.
I have a hard time experiencing the fullness of this moment.
I'll practice, and one day I'll stay here for all
    the fullness.
And, at that moment it will be enough …
    finally enough!

Palm Trees

- Rita Russell, M.A.W.E. -

*I*t was so tiny – less than an inch tall. I had almost forgotten about the palm tree that was painted on my big toenail. But it sure caught David's eye! And that little palm tree changed our lives!

Let me back up a bit …

In June 2002, I spent two weeks in Costa Rica on a mission trip. Only an hour from the Pacific Ocean, we had a couple of brief R & R's at the beach at midday, when it was too hot to do roof work and painting. inland. The beauty was incredible! The coolness of the water and gentle breezes were so welcome after the 110-degree temperatures in which we had been working.

On our last night, when our host offered personalized pedicures to the female team members, a palm tree seemed an appropriate choice for me. I would symbolically take a little bit of Costa Rica back home to Kentucky; each time I looked at that palm tree upon my return, I would be "taken back" to this beautiful country and its awesome people.

Less than two weeks after my return to the states, a friend called to see if I could join her and her husband in celebrating the birthday of their lifelong friend. I jumped at the chance for a free meal, a chance to show off pictures of Costa Rica … and a chance to get further acquainted with their (single, male) friend, whom I had met two months earlier. And it was after that free meal, as I was showing the pictures, that David happened to see my toes … and the palm tree … peeking above my sandals. In September, after we started officially dating, David told me that when he saw the toenails, he knew I was an interesting lady that he wanted to get to know better. On our wedding day in November (yes, after only three months of dating!), my toe-nails again had palm trees on them as I slipped a wedding band, engraved with a palm tree, on David's finger.

Who would have dreamed that a little thing like a palm tree on my big toe would be the catalyst for an awesome relationship between two soul mates? How could anyone know that we would both be rekindled with hope, love and joy as we became a couple after long years of singleness? I sure didn't know, but I'm glad that I went to Costa Rica and in a moment of fun was inspired by a palm tree. And I'll forever be grateful that the same Heavenly Father who put me on the path to share Jesus Christ in another country used a piece of that experience to put me on another path with a lifelong partner!

Discerning the Difference Between Disasters and Blessings

- Bob Vanderberry, M.D. -

*A*s I approach my 60th birthday, it has become increasingly apparent to me that my life is none of my business. Many of the things that I thought would be so wonderful haven't turned out that way, and the things that seemed like nightmares have proven to be character builders. The old adage that "hindsight is 20/20" is certainly true for me. The fact that growth and development continue to occur from birth to death is true. Four events in my life have shaped the way I have responded to the world. Only time will tell if those responses were reasonable. The true assessment may have to be made by my children, grandchildren, great-grandchildren and those I'll never know.

On a hot summer day I left for Fort Caswell, on the coast of North Carolina, to attend camp. I had just celebrated my ninth birthday. The camp's centerpiece was an old Civil War fortress with its underground bunkers and cannon placements. Within an hour of completing the 200-mile trip from home to the ocean, I was underground exploring the fortress with my buddies. There was one flashlight for five or six of us and I became separated from my friends. In the pitch dark and alone, I fearfully groped along the walls until I saw daylight. As I scrambled out of the cave, I saw my mother standing at the mouth of the tunnel. She informed me that my father had died. My world fell apart. To this day I still believe it was a disaster, but something good did come from it. As an only child, I had to grow up fast. By cutting grass, having a paper route and working at a service station, I learned to converse with all types of people. I also became handy at home by fixing plumbing, painting, and doing general maintenance. I was fortunate to have wonderful role models in my Boy Scout leaders. My father's death forced me to be more self-reliant.

Throughout my high school years, I pointed toward one goal: to win a specific, prestigious scholarship to the University of North Carolina. That scholarship required academic achievement, athletic ability, and leadership. I believed I had all the bases covered and had many successes in school, on the football field, in the community and in scouting. Unfortunately, the nomination went to another person from my school and I lost out. It seemed like a disaster at the time. I had some money left to me from my father, but not enough to finish college and medical school. Nevertheless, I was determined as I waited tables and sold advertising for the school newspaper at the University of North Carolina. The self-reliance and determination learned from age nine carried me through. It was also a case of using my anger constructively. I finished college and medical school owing very little in student loans. Marriage and two children soon followed. I completed my training as a pediatrician shortly after my second child's birth.

While serving as a career medical officer in the US Navy in 1980, I was given the opportunity to attend a two-week course for healthcare professionals on the recognition of alcoholism and other addictive diseases. This session was held at the Alcohol Rehabilitation Service at the Naval Hospital, San Diego, California. Prior to taking that course, I had been seeing multiple doctors for a myriad of medical problems. Having agreed not to drink alcohol during the doctors' course, I was surprised how much better I felt with each passing day. After one-and-a-half weeks, the scales were lifted from my eyes and I discovered I already had a degree in that course! My two-week stint turned into six-and-a-half weeks, as I reluctantly agreed to stay for treatment for my addiction. I really felt like a failure, despite my degrees and my accomplishments. Surprisingly enough, what seemed to be the biggest disaster of my life turned out to be the biggest blessing. By working the steps of recovery, I was able to overcome grief and abandonment issues that stemmed from my childhood. My obsessive-compulsive personality had helped me accomplish a great deal externally, but inside I was a lonely, untrusting, fearful person hiding behind my degrees. After 22 years of sobriety, I'm still not "cured" and never expect to be. I have learned that I'm just a fallible human being.

On a bright, sunny morning in April 1989, I was informed by my wife of over 24 years that she no longer needed me in her life's plans. Having come through what I thought was a disaster nine years earlier, I thought my life and that of my family was back on track. The new revelation on that spring morning rocked everything I believed in. As a pediatrician, I was arrogantly dead-set against the divorces I'd seen in the families whose children had been my patients. For me to get a divorce went against every fiber of my being, particularly since my own parents divorced when I was age six. At any rate, I felt like a hypocrite and a failure. Despite ten months of counseling, there was no hope of salvaging the marriage. A divorce ensued. When it was all over, I had lost 20 pounds and was back to my high school "playing weight." However, I was far from fit mentally. After a while, I decided to go back to church, from which I had been absent for a number of years. It was through the Singles Again group at church that I met a beautiful, spiritually-fit lady. We began dating and I was later invited to the wedding of one of her daughters. It seemed like such a good idea that we were married in 1991. All of our adult children then followed suit, with a wedding each year for five straight years! Now there are six grandchildren, and I don't think we're through yet.

So what's been learned? There are a number of things that come to mind and I'm sure none of them are original ideas. Here are some of the things that help me stay rekindled:

1. If everything is going well, you've obviously overlooked something.
2. Things generally work out the way they are supposed to, but rarely as you envision them.
3. If you are determined to be a "list maker," tackle the tough 20% first, and the rest will flow easier.
4. There's always unfinished business.
5. God can see further ahead than you can.
6. If you pray, don't worry. If you worry, don't pray.
7. God likes to hear from strangers.
8. Follow the First Rule of Holes – when you're in one, quit digging.
9. More is learned in the valleys of life than from the mountain-top experiences.
10. When disasters come your way, look for the lesson to be learned, and realize tincture of time is a wonderful balm for life's curve balls.

Spiritual Toolbox

- Alton Jamison -

*W*hen you think of what's in a toolbox, you think of things like a hammer, pliers, nails, etc. People tend to put things in a toolbox that they know they will need and use. A toolbox is a central location for all of the basic tools in one's workshop. Understanding this, translate it into the spiritual realm. What do you have in your spiritual toolbox? Do you have everything you need in order to survive? Here are some suggestions of things that you might want to keep handy in your spiritual toolbox:

Prayer (Hammer)

Prayer is considered the hammer of your spiritual toolbox. If nothing else, every toolbox has a hammer. The hammer is the universal tool for any worker. Prayer is the universal tool for anyone who is trying to grow spiritually. Prayer is a definite must if you want your toolbox to be complete.

Studying (Wrench)

Studying your Bible is considered the wrench of the toolbox. With a wrench, one can grab hold of something and either tighten or loosen it as he or she pleases. By studying your Bible, you can grab hold of the things in your life you need to tighten up on or the things you need to let go of or loosen.

Church (Screw Driver)

Church is considered the screwdriver of the toolbox. A screwdriver is a tool used to put the finishing touches on something, by making the final adjustments necessary for the object to be complete. This is the objective of attending church. Church helps to put the finishing touches on your spiritual growth. Church is also a place to go when you feel that you have become *spiritually loose* and need to be *retightened.*

Giving (Measuring Tape)

Giving is defined as the measuring tape of the toolbox. *For it is better to give than to receive (Acts 20:35).* Your level of giving to others is a measuring tape of the type of person you are, both spiritually and naturally. Every time you give, it measures your compassion and sincerity for others.

> *I have learned to appreciate the smallest things in life and take very little for granted, because life truly is a gift. I can only hope and pray that, with the decisions I make, I can impact those individuals who stand before me in a positive way.*
> *- Judge Kristin Ruth*

'Show' Not Tell

- Ann Wright -

I used to think being a career woman and making decisions affecting hundreds, perhaps thousands, of people a day was challenging and quite stressful at times. Little did I know that it was only preparing me for my most important, not to mention most challenging, and certainly most rewarding career – that of being a Mom.

Ever wonder how you talk or act? Watch how your child talks and acts. Ever wonder what you value? Watch what your children value.

One of the biggest challenges – in my career and more importantly, with my children – is how I can teach the really important things in life. You know: the intangibles, those values that were taught to you by your parents or mentors. Many things I value, such as honesty, integrity, determination, hard work, common courtesy, and respect are tough things to teach.

Remember how in kindergarten we all had the chance to bring something to "show and tell?" I have discovered that *showing*, not the *telling,* is perhaps the best way to teach the many values that are vital to becoming a good solid citizen. These values are more easily taught – or should I say learned – by observing (actions), as opposed to just being told how to act (words).

Though I have been a Mom only three short years, I have learned life-long lessons in helping Noah, my son, grow. Here are a few lessons that may help you, not only if you are raising children, but for your own growth and development!

Manners and Common Courtesy

One day, at a play area, I made sure that Noah said *please* and *thank-you* when asking another mom for some snacks. She made the comment that I couldn't expect a two-year-old to say *please* and *thank-you*. With a surprised look, I replied, "Well he does." Noah says *please* and *thank-you* now 99 percent of the time, without prompting, because it is expected of him. Not only do my husband, Doug, and I say *please* and *thank-you* to each other, but also to him. I believe children learn how to treat people by observing how other people – especially those who are influential in their lives – treat each other, and by how they are treated. Parents who want to command respect must show their children respect.

Mistakes

Oh, how difficult it is, and how many of us just cringe at the thought of having to admit we made a mistake. We want our children to have faith in us, believing we have all the answers. They need to know we're human and it's okay to be wrong, to admit you made a mistake.

Years ago I corrected a child because I thought she had taken something. I found out within the hour that she had in fact not taken the item. As hard as it was (not that it should have been) I sat down and told her I was very sorry and that adults make mistakes, and I had made one.

Noah, every once in awhile will say, "I'm sorry, it was my fault." He sounds just like me.

Determination and Hard Work

Sometimes one of the hardest things a parent must do is watch their child struggle. Noah recently broke his leg in an accidental fall. He was in a full lower body cast for five and a half weeks. At three, he is experiencing for the second time those milestones that a child usually experiences between 10 and 16 months. He has had to re-learn how to roll himself over, crawl, stand, climb stairs and walk. At the present time, he is still working on learning to walk. It would be very easy to carry him from room to room or up the stairs when asked; it would certainly be a lot faster to get from place to place. However, it would have taken him twice as long to learn again if we had done everything for him.

One of the hardest moments came in February when he struggled to climb the stairs. His challenges brought tears to my eyes, first in watching him struggle to make it up the stairs with me right behind him, and then when he made it up the stairs by himself. One of the most rewarding and proudest moments for my husband and me is when Noah says, "Mom (or Dad), look what I did" or "Look what I CAN do." Helping to instill a sense of independence, pride in what one accomplishes, and that "can do" attitude is important for children, so they can take it with them into adulthood.

Faith

Doug and I are also working to teach Noah the importance of Faith. Faith is hard enough for adults to understand, let alone a child. We are starting small, but working to help Noah form lifelong habits. It's all in how you frame it. Noah doesn't *have* to go to church – he *gets* to go to church. He loves making the sign of the cross, and even genuflects before he goes into the pew. We thank God before every meal and pray before bedtime. Noah even says, "God bless you" after people sneeze.

These are only a few of the many important life lessons that we are working to "show, not tell" Noah. The same lessons apply to the workplace: if you want people to behave in a certain way, you have to model that behavior. Maybe, just maybe, they'll catch on. It's working with Noah.

Give Me Some Kind of Sign, Will You?

- Mark Drury -

I have been on a weight loss program for about two years now and Lord knows it is a tough road to hoe at times. I sure can use all the help I can get. I have recently begun to notice that God really wants me to succeed at this for some reason. He has recently started sending me what I refer to as "signs."

Now I'm not talking about signs like Mel Gibson's corn crops in his hit movie, *Signs*. I am talking about those times when I have just about had it up to here. Several times a week I think that I am just going to scream if I have to peel one more dried-out chicken breast off my George Foreman grill.

I like to eat out at restaurants a few times a week to break the monotony. I will be sitting there all hot and bothered at Tony Romas with thoughts of taking a breather from the diet regime and ordering me a big old Onion Ring Loaf and a rack of baby back ribs to lift my spirits. Then straight from heaven above, the hostess will sit two guys right across from my booth that weigh 350 pounds apiece. I now call this "my sign." It happens every time – without fail. I am always seated near several morbidly obese people in every restaurant situation. The service person shows up to take my order and I take the "advice from above" and order the grilled salmon, dry baked potato, and broccoli. Unsweetened tea to drink. Put the Corona back in the fridge. Give that onion ring loaf to somebody else. I will just lick the picture of the baby back ribs on the back of the menu. I am on a mission. I got "the sign."

"The sign" has begun to appear in other places. I will sit down with a bowl of popcorn, turn on WTBS Superstation and here sits John Goodman in a scene with Roseanne Arnold on the old "Roseanne" sitcom. I put the popcorn away.

In the grocery I will decide to buy a bag of chips and around the corner comes "the sign." The chips go back on the shelf. My life is turning into *The Twilight Zone*.

I took my mother to a local seafood restaurant on the scenic Ohio River one Saturday night last November. She is very aware of "the sign" and looks for it whenever she is with me in a restaurant. We were on the raised mezzanine in the restaurant. I was really hungry for some fried fish, and theirs is the best. All around the mezzanine, there were approximately 100 diners. There was not a single overweight person in the whole place – not even one person with more than 10 pounds to lose. Just 100 or so hungry people eating batter-fried shrimp, onion rings, hushpuppies, and fried fish, while watching a big screen television tuned to ESPN. I could not believe it. "The sign" was no place to be seen. God had taken the night off. As the waitress approached the table, my mother pointed it out to me.

"Mark, look at the television screen!" she said, pointing her finger.

Right there, big as the nose on your face, was the ESPN coverage of the Japanese Sumo Wrestling Championships from the MGM Grand in Las Vegas. Two big 500-pound guys in diapers trying to knock one another out of a circle.

I ordered the broiled cod and water, and asked her to bring me the remote control.

How to Be Happy
Without Spending a Cent

- Judy Payne -

*W*hether our own children and our self-indulgent society want our help or not, it seems to me that our most loving legacy is the wisdom we have gleaned from our own life's lessons. I offer here a bit of my perspective in the hope it will help you clarify what success and happiness mean to you and how you might try to leave the world a tad better place than you found it.

First, My Observations and Conclusions

As you watched the relatives and friends of 9/11 victims being interviewed on TV, did you notice a common theme in their responses? Over and over I heard bereaved folks say they were sure that *their* loved one died helping someone else, or that a void was created because of some strength of character *their* departed one took from this world. I didn't hear anyone mention the deceased's high salary or wheeler/dealer power, fancy car, athletic prowess, or gorgeous body. Hmm. Is there a lesson here about what – deep down – we already *know* constitutes a successful, happy life?

These comments validate my beliefs concerning the human condition from my vantage point as a mom, teacher, speaker, writer and loser of 110 pounds twenty-some years ago. I think there must be something in our DNA that allows us to feel truly happy only when the following intrinsic conditions prevail:

◆ We work hard to do our best with the many or few natural abilities we were given, and

◆ We aspire to be primarily givers, not takers.

If my hunch is right, no wonder our old extrinsic formula for success and happiness isn't working for us. Rather, we live in a S.A.D (Selfish, Angry, Dumb) Society of semi-miserable people in a frantic quest for extrinsic fun instead of intrinsic happiness. We seek to acquire the extrinsic symbols of success and expect these trophies to somehow fulfill our spiritual, intrinsic need to feel happy.

There are oodles of people who appear to "have it all," but feel unsatisfied because society's superficial definitions of success and happiness have failed them. So how do we, as individuals and as a society, realign our goals with what we intuitively know is real success and the key to true happiness?

It's simple – not easy, but simple. We need to replace our current "King Midas Law" for success and happiness, with what I will humbly call "Judy's Law." All I did was revise the formulas a bit to do two things:

- ◆ **Redefine** success and happiness to reflect what we all know would rekindle the spirit in all of us.
- ◆ **Re-evaluate** our methods for evaluating success and happiness.

The Old "King Midas' Law" Formula
Result: Extrinsic, Short-Term, Phony Success and Happiness

Step 1:
$$M^\wedge + P^\wedge + S^\wedge = SU$$
Translation: Lots of money + lots of power + lots of stuff = Success

Step 2:
$$SU + F = H$$
Translation: Success + Fun = Happiness

The New "Judy's Law" Formula
Result: Intrinsic, Long-Term, Genuine Success and Happiness

Step 1:
(Here I added the old, forgotten, vital ingredient-**STRUGGLE**)
    $ST = (S+K)+(SE)+(SC)+C$
Translation: STRUGGLE = skills and knowledge + self esteem + self confidence + character

Step 2:
Therefore: $ST=SU$
Translation: Struggle=Success

Step 3:
Consequently: $SU=H$
Translation: Success=Happiness

How To Implement "Judy's Law"

Goal: Happy Humans and Harmonious Humanity

◆ First, look at your own life and listen to your own heart! Take note of the superficiality, the impossibility to control, and the minimal short-term satisfaction you get from your consuming, socially-expected, extrinsic activities and rewards.

◆ Next, flip your mind over and think about the unacknowledged, long-term joy, pleasure and satisfaction you receive from your growing, loving, unheralded, intrinsic activities and accomplishments.

◆ Finally, be sure you know the difference between extrinsic, short-term fun, and intrinsic, long-term happiness.

Did that personal 3-step examination give you a wake-up call about the ridiculous Madison Avenue and Wall Street definitions of success and happiness that you have just accepted through osmosis? If so, simply do the following:

- **Stop** letting others determine how you feel about yourself (extrinsic). I've noticed that people who know this are already happy, even if they aren't rich, trouble-free, smart or beautiful.
- **Start** putting more quiet time, growth experiences, challenging tasks, delayed gratification and service to others into your life.

How To Pass It On

Raising and educating kids and saving our S.A.D Society could be much easier if we incorporated some old conscience-building motivators that have been disappearing over the last couple of generations. In addition to avoiding struggle in our quest for ease, equity, and absolutes, we have also omitted healthy portions of fear, guilt, fairness, and common sense. Thank goodness we aren't so morally numb that we no longer care if people are devoid of conscience. We evidence some moral outrage by our willingness to spend oodles on the law to pursue and punish slackers for their lack of character. It sure would be a lot cheaper if adults would just model, teach, and enforce good character in children until their copycatting becomes a repertoire of habits and behavior. Then, ideally, both kids and adults would automatically practice good character – even when no one is watching.

Perhaps, in order to help our self-absorbed, angry, adrenaline-addicted kids learn how to make themselves happy, we could start with the following:

1. Take back control of our children.
- We have rich and poor spoiled kids who are allowed to make too many decisions for themselves, with

too much discretionary time and money to spend without adult guidance.

◆ We adults are shirking our responsibility to model responsible decision-making and set boundaries.

◆ Discipline should be a learning experience, not just punishment; it should be administered out of love, not frustration.

◆ Our kids need more opportunities to be givers. They flourish when helping one another. (This I know because I studied it in my own classroom for years. The payback for the teacher is that kids learn at far higher levels, and discipline problems are rare.)

2. *Talk about character and honor at home, school, and in the workplace.*

◆ If a child indicates she/he would like to be an accountant, focus on the positive choices in which to use that career, such as working for a cancer research foundation.

◆ The writings of our forefathers are rich with examples of how they made honor and dignity top priorities in their personal and public lives. Talk about these guys, as well as everyday heroes and heroines.

◆ Consider having every family member create a mission statement. It could even become a big deal, with a special family ceremony.

3. *Model and expect good character.*

◆ Instill habits of good behavior and character by modeling and expecting good manners, saving money, delaying gratification, and offering service to others.

4. Reevaluate how we evaluate kids.

◆ Isn't struggling to be the best we can be, the best we can do?

◆ Schools should incorporate into their grading philosophies at least *some* concept demonstrating that the biggest reward for learning is not the extrinsic grade, but the intrinsic joy of learning.

Have you ever noticed that in the long-term, we don't respect teachers who gave us that "Easy A?" Instead, we respect the teacher who pushed us and made us struggle to be our best.

◆ Too often, schools count what is countable, but not necessarily what counts. For accountability, schools depend upon one-size-fits-all, right/wrong, win/lose, quantitative and easily calculated answers. Outside the classroom, we wouldn't expect a 4-foot kid to "beat" a 6-foot kid on a basketball court. We wouldn't give a baby a bad grade because he doesn't learn to walk the same day other babies his age learned to walk. Instead, we let him rise and fall until he masters the learning.

We may have umpteen types of intelligences identified now, but some kids just have more of them than others do. I've seen kids try hard, but eventually give up because they know they will never "succeed" by the school's definition of success.Why not create a variety of opportunities to showcase each child's special gift?

◆ Kids will do anything to avoid looking stupid. Difficulty with learning is the elephant in the middle of the living room. Our society tries to force everyone to look smart and believes that money, power, and stuff are the evidence. Let's focus instead on the intangibles that mean the most.

Now It's Your Turn.

Please try to improve upon my ideas and add your own. Although we will never get it exactly "right," the good news is that all we have to do to be successful and happy is do our best to raise successful, happy kids. This will improve our S.A.D.Society. The process *is* the product. The bottom line is:

The STRUGGLE will make us SUCCESSFUL and HAPPY.

(Artwork by Colleen Fire Thunder)

The Power of the Heart

- Edie Raether, M.S., CSP -

*R*ekindling is a gift that cannot be forced or contrived. It comes from the heart, in spontaneous and generous behaviors. I would like to share two true stories that exemplify the powerful and spontaneous nature of rekindling.

At a time when there is often great suspicion and distrust between employer and employee, this story portrays a loyalty beyond belief. When all precautions and proper procedures are taken to protect our most valuable asset, our workers, true accidents may still happen. Such was the case in a worksite accident when a conscientious laborer was diligently about his work and in one brief moment, lost his finger. The trauma of the event was experienced by more than the hard-working employee and his immediate colleagues, friends and family. A most humble, concerned and compassionate CEO demonstrated the ultimate in altruism, asking the surgeon if his own finger might be amputated and given to his employee, stating, "That man needs his finger to make a living ... I don't."

Have you ever found the perfect suit? One that the designer, through some kind of cosmic connection, made just for you. The cut, the fit, the fabric all reek ... YOU! And as you try it on, everyone in the boutique says, "That suit was made for you. You can't go home without it."

Obstacle number one – the price! With the influence of a German, Lutheran mother who had experienced the Great Depression, I have vivid recall of recycling "everything" long before it was fashionable, and having a dress made from the 50-pound flour sack. As a result, my modus operandi is to only purchase clothes when they are at least 80 percent off. Besides, Goodwill and the Salvation Army now feature designer specials for the cost of one button on the suit.

So, although the onlookers in the shopper's choir chant, "Get it, get it, get it," past programming persists, and after hours of deliberation between your id and super ego, you leave your identity on the hanger and walk out with pangs of separation anxiety.

Such was the scenario when I entered *Tina Marie's*, my favorite boutique in my hometown of Algoma, Wisconsin. Tina is a bubbly, genuine, flamboyant blonde who could sell pork chops in Israel ... but she could not sell me!!! Her first defeat, I'm sure.

Six months later, I returned to her boutique asking if she might sell my book, *Why Cats Don't Bark*, knowing she would outperform Barnes and Noble and Borders. After delivering several boxes of books – she always thinks "big" – I searched her shop for the suit no one would dare buy without a karmic revenge. It screamed at me from the back room, like a dog seeking its master. The reunion with "the suit" was tender and touching, but still without a sale. To purchase anything not on sale would be a violation of the soul, at least mine. Again I began a mediation of the minds, but history has its pull, and I could only think of how much $600 would buy in flour sacks, grass seed and detergent. The romance was still there, the chemistry was strong, but old habits are hard to break.

My struggle between the intense desire for the suit and the unwillingness to pay its price was obvious to Tina. Keep in mind this is a woman with whom I had always resonated, but we had not had an opportunity to really get to know each other. We had never even shared coffee or lunch. This wonderful woman watched my inner battle, then asked if I had a bit of room in my suitcase to take something back with me. With a sparkle in her eye, she wrapped up "the perfect suit" and insisted I accept this most generous gift, refusing any payment.

As I drove to the airport with tears rolling down my cheeks, I was emotionally numb and stunned by her genuine, spontaneous giving to an instant soul mate.

These true stories give me such hope for humankind. We hear so many news stories and read so many articles about the "bad guys;" it is so refreshing to be reminded that, as Ann Frank wrote in her diary, "… in spite of everything, I still believe that people are really good at heart." There are so many folks out there who truly do care, and these stories of spontaneous giving are symbols of the many caring, unselfish people who, by their daily actions, provide a perpetual rekindling of the human spirit.

When you feel inspired to spontaneously give from your heart, do not hesitate! You never know whose heart and soul you are rekindling!

The Facets of Friendship

- Carey Hill, M.A. -

What a lovely thing to be
given a friend,
A person to know my heart,
One on whom I can depend,
In my life plays a purposeful part.

My friend is a child God has lent me,
A tool and a gift to enjoy,
Handled carefully, gratefully
she must be,
Not treated as a simple toy.

The life of a friendship
like flower or tree,
Takes work and watering to root,
But with care as it ages all
are able to see,
Its beauty of color and fruit.

Yes, as friendship grows
and deepens,
I'm molded and sharpened
and changed,
Unlimited benefits, blessings
to reap,
I feel almost rearranged.

A friendship shows God's love is real,
That He really has arms and a smile,
Through the warmth of a friend
God's comfort I feel,
Like sitting in His lap for a while.

And thanks for our similarities and
differences,
Of character and interests and looks.
Help me appreciate this richness,
Like opening an exciting new book.

In my friend I can see a reflection,
Of myself–for the good and the bad,
Each day's a new challenge
to change and grow,
No matter what failures I've had.

Help me to be as an image of You,
In their lives every time that we meet,
Close friends, true friends
are so very few,
When we're together let me walk in
Your feet.

Thanks for my friends, these stars
You have sent,
I'm grateful for the old
and the new,
They guide, enlighten, and
brighten my life,
Just like a visit from You.

And when it's time for change ... to part,
My sister, my friend, and I,
What a joy to remember we're
joined at the heart,
In Your Spirit we can't say goodbye.

The "Power2Choose"

- Dana C. Foster -

As I look back at my life and recount the events that led me to where I am today, I realize that it all boils down to the various choices I've made over the years. While I didn't get to pick the era in which I was born (the 60s), nor the particular place on the planet (Ohio), most of those years I was the pilot of this human vessel known as me.

Along the way I faced many problems, politics, and positively ludicrous relationships. Of course there were some tremendously good times as well, but if I had the chance to do it all again, I would have used the power of choice in a better fashion.

During my career as a salesperson, I faced a major reorganization within the company I worked for. In order to keep a position with the company, I was forced to move to a lower position and another place in the country. The situation took a tremendous toll on my family and me. We were extremely happy living in a town with only 23,000 people, but now we had to adjust to a town with more than 3 million. I truly felt defeated, but because this job was our only source of income, I had to somehow learn to accept this change and move forward.

Over time, however, something inside me said that although this was the hand life dealt me, it was up to me to decide just how to play it. So I made a choice: I would never be placed in this type of situation again, by having just one source of income. In time I developed several ways to generate other streams of legitimate income. Therefore, if one source went south or ended, the others would carry us through until we found another.

It wasn't long before I replaced the income from my position with the company, and was able to tell them good-bye and wish them well. It was one of the best choices I ever made. No longer could their choices affect my family and me. It took me quite some time to discover that, out of all the powers given to us, the power of choice has to be the greatest.

> *If I had the chance to do it all again, I would have used the power of choice in a better fashion.*

With this knowledge now well in hand, whenever I am faced with any outside force – either positive or negative, good or evil, problem or opportunity, pain or pleasure – I will control, through the power of choice, how or if it will affect me. Furthermore, with this newly discovered power, I have become a more proactive and action-oriented person. Life is much too short to be mainly reactive, just waiting for things in your life to appear. I set all the goals now, choose the directions, actions and amount of self-discipline necessary to obtain my desired outcomes.

Although there are still many politics, negative situations, and difficult choices to make, by finally recognizing how tremendous the power of choice is, I am prepared to face whatever life brings. All I can say is, I hope you discover and learn to actively use this great power God divinely chose to give us all: the Power of Choice.

The Power of Vision:
From Down Under Dreams to Lone Star Livin'
- Theresa Behenna -

*Y*ou've heard it all before. "You get what you ask for." "If you can see it and believe it, you can achieve it." Yeah, right. So how come I'm not living happily ever after in a palace with Prince Charming who, by the way, is handsome, successful, romantic AND loves to cook? And YOU might ask yourself, "How come I'm stuck in a rut at work, 10 pounds overweight and have to deal with a couch potato husband and three video-addicted kids?"

The answer is simple according to Stephen Covey. In *The Seven Habits of Highly Effective People,* he notes about envisioning our future, "Begin with the end in mind." Well, d-u-h. What does THAT mean?

I'm from the land Down Under. Back in my youth I didn't know a thing about visualizing my future, let alone having a mental picture of my life, my career or Mr. Right. Furthermore, I'm from Adelaide, South Australia. That's important because Adelaide is very similar to a lot of small towns in America. Everyone knows everyone else. Everyone knows everyone else's business. Nobody ever leaves, unless, of course, they're running for public office. However, when I was growing up there as a little girl I had an ongoing dream about traveling around the world to exotic places. I wanted to be different. I wanted to be special. I wanted people to notice me, big time! The only problem was: I didn't have the foggiest idea how I was going to do that.

My Mother often used to catch me in our back yard all dressed up in a little Wild West outfit complete with guns and cowboy hat. There I was, pretending to be on a stage, bowing before an invisible audience. Now here's where it

255

gets weird. I was singing a song called "Deep In the Heart of Texas." I didn't even know where Texas was! Yet at eight years old, I was gung-ho on playing cowboys and Indians while all the other little girls were playing with Barbie dolls. Talk about 'vision by default!' because here I am now living 'Deep In the Heart of Texas' – Houston! Not only that, but I have traveled around the world and lived in ten other countries. In addition, for the past 20 years I've been on the stage as a professional pianist. All my childhood visions became my reality! (I still enjoy playing with cowboys too, but I'm not going there in this article!)

We can all shape our own future if we deliberately choose what we want. We can picture the end result and start from there.

Where do YOU see yourself in 10 years? Or even one year? Be careful what you wish for. I'm here to tell all of y'all that we eventually get exactly what we ask for – whether we recognize it or not. It's called vision and here is how it works: whatever we repeatedly focus on and talk about we attract into our lives. People who constantly speak about lack, limitation, illness and negativity experience more of the same. We are constantly reaping the results of our thoughts and words.

Today I've changed from the musical stage to the speaking stage. Did I ever realize the powerful impact of my words and dreams as a kid? No! Am I careful about what I say and envision these days? You'd better believe it! I'm going to be more than just a "survivor of the outback."

How about you?

A Ray of Hope

- Cher Holton -

It's amazing how a little thing can make a dramatic difference in your attitude! I have always considered myself to be a very positive person. But even the most positive person in the world has down times, and needs a bit of rekindling.

Following the tragedy of September 11, 2001, we were experiencing a rather difficult time with our business, as were a lot of self-employed individuals in the speaking profession. After a while, the unreturned calls, cancelled dates and empty calendar got the best of me, and I was in the depths of one of those "dark night of the soul" moments, wondering what the point was to anything. I truly felt hopeless, not sure what to do next.

Early one morning, as I was lying in bed writing in my journal, putting my depression into words on the page, my husband, Bil, came running into the room.

"Honey! You've got to come out to the kitchen – quick!"

Now you have to realize that Bil is fabulous in honoring my morning journal time. In fact, he typically brings me a cup of wonderful, freshly-brewed gourmet flavored coffee, to help me kick-start my morning! So of course I was a little startled by his boisterous announcement! And I noticed he did not have a cup of coffee in his hand! I knew something major was up!

I jumped out of bed and followed him into the kitchen. With a sparkle in his eye, he pointed to the sink and said, "Look down into the drain."

I walked over to the sink and gazed into the inky darkness of the kitchen sink drain. Not seeing anything earth-shaking or mysterious, I looked back up at Bil with a quizzical look on my face. He said, "Keep looking – and watch this!"

As I stared down into the pitch black darkness of the drain, Bil reached down and opened the cabinet door positioned right under the sink. To my amazement, the drain lit up as if a 150-watt light bulb had been turned on. Bil shut the door, and the drain was dark again. He opened the door, and the light flooded it.

Here's what was happening. The sunlight was flooding into our kitchen through one of our windows, positioned so that when the cabinet door opened, it hit the door in such a way that the sunbeam reflected onto the plastic drain pipe under the sink, thus creating vivid and bright light through the drain. When the door was shut, it blocked the light to the drain, and darkness prevailed.

This became a Marker Moment in my life! The analogy was obvious to me. So often things look absolutely dark. That is when we reach a point of hopelessness. Without hope, we lose the light and muddle in the darkness. But what we need to realize is that the light is there – God is there. We just need to open the door, and what seemed dark will suddenly and brilliantly be flooded with light. When I made the connection, I felt a resurgence of hope flow through my very soul!

As I reflect on what I've come to label *The Sink Drain Phenomenon*, I recognize that there are three critical elements in rekindling hope. I call it the T.A.P. theory.

Timing

It was important to view the kitchen sink drain at the right moment. Other times, the sun would not be reflecting at just the correct angle to create the vision we observed. Timing is also critical as we renew that flame of hope. When you feel depressed, it is easy to wallow in the negative emotions, and second guess everything. It is important to take advantage of opportunities when they come. Even though you may question your intuition, believe in it and follow your thoughts. They arrive at just the right moment, and if you over-analyze them, you will miss your best opportunities.

Action

We had to open the cabinet door to see the light. Even though the light was there all the time, some action was required to create the brightness. In our moments of darkest despair, it is invaluable to take action. Even if you don't know what to do, it is important to do something! Move your feet, and you will be guided to solutions you never realized were there. Take the action, and the darkness will become light.

Perspective

Once I experienced the *Sink Drain Phenomenon*, my entire perspective changed. I felt a renewal within my very soul, and hope flowed through my spirit. At that moment, I was reminded how powerful hope is. I suddenly had more energy, felt lighter and viewed our situation with a different vision. In the twinkling of an eye, my entire perspective changed. And with the change in perspective came new ideas, new attitudes, new solutions.

When you face your own "dark night of the soul," I encourage you to remember the *Sink Drain Phenomenon*. Remember there is light just waiting to flood into your soul, bringing ideas, energy and hope to you. You just need to open the door, and let the light shine in!

Beyond the Mountain

- Edie Raether, M.S., CSP -

*A*fter I've climbed the mountain and reached the top, I look down and reminisce the struggle – the encounters, the drives, and the great sense of achievement in saying "I've made it."

I look where I've been and look where I've arrived and question myself with "What next?" Life still is – and "I" still am, but the top has been reached.

There's only me and the universe, which is intangible, difficult to define, grab on to, or hold. But I need something; something out there or something in me, for the mountain I possess, but the universe never becomes ours. It does not support nor hold us as the mountain, but it does provide a mystical experience, an enlightenment which can only "be" from the top of the mountain when the struggle is over, and one is free to experience that which "is."

In the climb, one does not have time nor energy for introspection and reflection, for in climbing we look upward and outward. But, when all that which lies ahead is behind us, our vision becomes introverted, and we discover the pleasure, excitement, and contentment which is ours – both a sense of peace and power which is within each of us, waiting to be explored. The spiritual communion of becoming one with the universe, with ourselves, and with each other is an elation and enlightenment beyond thoughts, words or comprehension. It is a reality of the senses, the feelings, and the higher powers which be. It can only be experienced to be known and understood. It is continually evolving, becoming, and changing, and thus does not repeat itself.

Each moment is unique, spontaneous, and a new creation. Each moment is – you are – and I am – together we exist, live, experience …
… beyond the mountain.

Meet Our Contributors:

Billy Arcement, M.Ed., author of *Searching for Success*, is a professional speaker and consultant specializing in developing leadership and management skills for business and government leaders. He teaches politically-free boardmenship that keeps children first with school board members. His website, www.searchingforsuccess.com contains information about his services.

Debra Atkinson, M.S., is a Personal and Business Coach. With over 18 years as a fitness professional, she operates her own personal training business and lectures at Iowa State University in Health and Human Performance. She is a national presenter, published author and speaker. Visit her website at www.lifetoogoodtobetrue.com.

Australian pianist **Theresa Behenna** is a humorous motivational speaker who specializes in winning communications using the power of words. Theresa plays a piano keyboard in her unique presentations that teach people how to achieve goals and reduce negativity in their lives. She can be contacted at theresatalks@pdq.net.

Ildeasela Buso is known as Tati among friends and coaching clients. She is a writer, personal coach and scientific information analyst. She is a member of the Ohio Trans Latina Women's Writing Workshop, a creative writing group focusing on ethnic and gender awareness, family reconstruction, and personal self-discoveries. (b.tati@lycos.com)

Van Carpenter, the Front Porch Philosopher, shares timeless wisdom, life experiences, and a large dose of Southern humor sprinkled liberally with tips, sources and motivation to enable you to develop or refine your own Front Porch Approach. Visit Van at www.frontporchphilosopher.com.

Dick Cheatham loves life and liberty, and pursues happiness through speaking and writing about them. A VMI graduate, former TV news correspondent, educator, historian and weekly newspaper columnist, Dick speaks all over the country portraying important American historical characters – Meriwether Lewis, Pocahontas' husband, President John Tyler and others. (dcheatham@LHALtd.com)

Lisa Church decided to apply years of Corporate Support experience in a new direction after suffering a miscarriage. She now offers support for women and their families coping with pregnancy loss. Her book and HopeXchange.com website will be coming soon to supply information, hope and healing. Contact Lisa at Lisa@hopeXchange.com.

261

Marty Clarke, owner of Martin Production and author of *Communication Land Mines! 18 Communication Catastrophes and How to Avoid Them*, draws enthusiastic audiences for his speeches and workshops. His interests include hockey, photography, reading and a passion for movies. Contact Marty at 919-518-0566, or online at www.martinproduction.com.

"Coach Bud" Coggins shares 40+ years experience to help his clients "Create, Develop and Grow A Successful Entrepreneurial Business." After a successful 20-year career in television broadcasting, with two children in college and one in high school, Bud was compelled to pursue his "passion" for independence. Please visit www.cogginsmarketing.com for information about "Coach Bud's" MarketingU.

www.BreathingSpace.com offers information of **Jeff Davidson**'s keynote speeches, including *Managing Information and Communication Overload* and *Prospering in a World of Rapid Change*. Other books include: *The Sixty-Second Procrastinator* (Adams Media); *Christian Family Guide to Organizing* (Penguin); *The Complete Idiot's Guide to Managing Your Time* (Alpha/Penguin); and *Breathing Space* (MasterMedia).

Brian Detrick is a lay speaker and Bible teacher, and is a member of both St. Paul's United Methodist Church in New Gretna, New Jersey, and Grace Community Church in Arlington, Virginia. He is a retired intelligence officer, and served in Vietnam in the U.S. Army.

Marguerite Detrick has a unique perspective on life, gained from 49 years as a minister's wife. She is now back in her native NJ, living in the house her father built the year she was born. She teaches an adult Sunday School class and enjoys reading, traveling and cooking. Contact Marguerite at 609-965-2129.

Mark Drury is a 47-year-old budding fitness enthusiast, professional speaker, humorist and survivor. Overcoming morbid obesity and heart surgery, he is a man with a new lease on life. You can learn more about Mark by going to www.markgetsitdone.com or www.bluegrassspeakersbureau.com.

Nancy Eubanks has been the Program Administrator for The Holton Consulting Group, Inc. since 1984. Her fun in life comes from her relationship with her granddaughters, as well as line dancing, singing, playing the piano and working crossword puzzles. Her strong family ties, friends and her faith in God make life exciting and worthwhile.

Colleen Fire Thunder is an artist and teacher in High Point, North Carolina. She is creator of the *Art is in the Eye*™ workshop, which teaches students to see the way artists see. She is also the creator of *Self*

Sovereignty: the Building Blocks of Integrity™, a workshop for teens. Email: C_firethunder@yahoo.com.

Summer Rose Fire Thunder is a nine-year-old home-schooled student who volunteers in the local elementary school by reading to younger children and working in the school library. She wants to help create positive social change and has a desire to protect the environment.

Dana Foster, MBA, President of Rventure Enterprises Inc., is a Professional Speaker and member of the National Speakers Association. He is also a published author with more than 18 years of business experience working within a $70 billion company. Dana also holds a US patent in the processing industry.

Scott Friedman, CSP specializes in humorous motivational talks on change, sales and service, and in teaching Corporate America how to use humor effectively in the workplace. He is the author of *Using Humor for a Change* and *Punchlines, Pitfalls and Powerful Programs*. Contact Scott at Scott@FunnyScott.com or through www.FunnyScott.com.

Faye E. Fulton, president of Training & Communicating, Inc., based in Houston, TX, helps people improve their communication skills and develop dynamic interpersonal skills. She specializes in grammar and business writing, presenting, working as a team, and negotiating. Contact Faye at 713 667-8907 or fefulton@ev1.net.

Lois J. Gallo is a Strategic Wealth Coach with Sagemark Consulting and author of *Million $ Planning: One Step at a Time*. She serves as President-Elect for the Financial Planning Association (Hampton Roads), is on the Board of the World Affairs Council, and is the Newsletter Editor for the National Speakers Association (Virginia Chapter).

Christina W. Giles resides in Pepperell, MA and has her own consulting firm in healthcare administration, focusing on medical staff administration and general management topics. She is a contributing author and editor to the *Handbook of Medical & Professional Staff Management, Third Edition*. Contact Chris at 978-433-2453 or chriswg@charter.net.

PBS TV calls **Susan Greene** the Communication Expert. TEC awarded her for delivery, content and tenure working with CEO roundtables internationally. She's a catalyst in facilitating executives, entrepreneurs, couples and individuals to build powerful relationships and organizations, and author of *The Most Important Conversation Is the One You're Not Having*. Info: www.communicatingworks.com or 713-782-2212.

Carol Hacker, M.S., is a human resource consultant, speaker and seminar leader who for the past 25 years has been a significant voice in front-line and corporate human resource management to small businesses as well as Fortune 100 companies. She's authored over 150 articles and 11 highly-acclaimed business books. Contact Carol at 770-410-0517 in Alpharetta, Georgia.

Joyce Williams Harris and her best friend, husband, and business partner, Bob, are owners of Joyce's Jewels, founded in 1992, featuring high Fashion jewelry and professional-image consulting. Her family is even more precious than jewels to her, and she and Bob are currently planning their next special memory. (joycesjewels@starfishnet.com)

Artomat artist, trainer, freelance writer and Sarah Lawrence graduate **Luba Havraniak, M.S.**, is originally from New York City, has lived in Paris, and currently resides in North Carolina. Her focus areas include inspiring creativity, communications, train the trainer, and customer service training. She can be reached at lubalh@yahoo.com.

Diana Hershberger has called Raleigh, NC home for 20 years. Although her struggle with depression has taken its toll, she maintains an interest in playing the guitar and reading. Her support network includes her roommate (who is like a sister), and her mother and three brothers who reside in Indiana.

Carey Hill, M.A., LPC, NCC, is president and owner of Carey Hill Consulting Inc., a Human Resource Consulting and Executive Coaching firm. She blends the experience of her 19-year career with the interpersonal acumen of a licensed professional, to bring a fresh perspective to every assignment she accepts. Contact Carey at careyhill@earthlink.net or 919-844-2920.

Janet Holliday-Cashwell, Ed.D., is a native of Eastern North Carolina. After teaching for 11 years, she has continued a service career in the private sector as a Human Resources Manager at Sprint for the last 13 years. She and her husband, Ronnie, and Maggie the cat, reside in Raleigh, NC. Janet may be contacted at jhc1313@bellsouth.net.

Professionally, **Bil Holton, Ph.D., GIR** is a nationally-recognized author, ghostwriter and publisher, ghosting for celebrities and well-known authors, speakers, trainers and consultants. Personally he enjoys competitive ballroom dancing with his wife, Cher; hanging out with his granddaughter, Mya; world travel; golf; writing; jigsaw puzzles; and retailing on eBay and amazon.com. Contact Bil at 800-336-3940 or www.holtonconsulting.com.

Cher Holton, Ph.D., CSP, CMC uniquely combines the skills of speaker, trainer, consultant and group facilitator into one dynamic bundle of energy. Cher is most requested for her TurboTraining™ and unique Just-In-Time Coaching™. She and her husband, Bil, are competitive ballroom dancers. Contact Cher at 800-336-3940, visit her website: www.holtonconsulting.com or e-mail cher@holtonconsulting.com.sp

Shari Hudson, The Master Organizer,^{SM} teaches individuals and businesses nuts and bolts techniques for getting and staying organized and helps them build P.E.P.^{SM}– Profitability, Energy and Productivity. Shari runs Organized by Design, in Adel, Iowa, and is a speaker, consultant, author and member of the National Association of Professional Organizers.

Ted Hurwitz is the Executive Director of the City University of New York Athletic Conference. In addition to his professional basketball playing career overseas, Ted has coached men's and women's basketball and tennis, served on numerous NCAA and ECAC committees, and been inducted into the Athletic Hall of Fame for both City College and Lehman.

Alton Jamison is a nationally recognized Youth Motivational Speaker specializing in youth empowerment, at-risk youth and leadership programs for young men. Alton is a graduate of Old Dominion University and is currently pursuing a Master of Arts in Practical Theology from Regent University. Contact Alton at 757-934-6878 or altonj@againstallodds.us.

As the president of Mannix & Associates, **Ursula Mannix** has made it her life's work to support the efforts of black, Asian, and Latin women to succeed in their personal and professional lives.

Diane L. Merriett's submission to *Rekindling the Human Spirit,* entitled "Each Day," signals her first foray into the arena of published writing under her own name. A marketing specialist by day and freelance writer by night, Diane resides in Washington, DC.

Janis Nark, Lt. Col., USAR (Ret.) served for 26 years in the Army Nurse Corps with assignments that included Vietnam and Desert Storm. Through her motivational speaking, she addresses the areas of change and stress with content, humor and scalpel-sharp insights for succeeding in today's chaotic world. Contact Janis at 828-652-5490, 828-674-8223 (cell), JanisNark@aol.com or www.nark.com.

Gail Ostrishko, a creative free spirit, specializes in nurturing individuals and organizations to tap into and radiate their internal wisdom through unique interactive learning adventures. A proud graduate of East Carolina University, Gail is a Licensed Professional Counselor and volunteer for the Make-A-Wish Foundation. Contact Gail at gail@GailO.com or call 919-779-2772.

Judy Payne is currently a happy, humorous, character education trainer. She is a former Golden Apple Award-winning high school teacher, college instructor, speaker, writer, business owner, and *Des Moines Sunday Register* columnist who lost 110 pounds 20+ years ago. Contact: 515-576-0877 or jpayne@dodgenet.com, or visit Judy's website: www.dodgenet.com/~jpayne.

A change strategist and Fortune 50 favorite, **Edie Raether, M.S., CSP** is an expert on innovative thinking and intuitive intelligence (the other IQ). As an international speaker, performance coach and author, Edie promises a positive ROI on your intellectual capital. View her live at www.raether.com or contact her at (919-557-7900) – edie@raether.com.

Ray Rimmer is founder and President of Corporate Excellence Outdoors, based in Greensboro, North Carolina. His mobile training and development programs have empowered tens of thousands of individuals, and shaped the positive identities of a thousand teams. Ray specializes in designing and using trust-building exercises, group initiatives, and high ropes elements.

Carla Royal, M.Ed., has been a psychotherapist in private practice for 12 years, helping to bring hope and healing to individuals, couples and families. Presently, while continuing her private practice, she is transitioning to a life of greater simplicity and creativity.

Rita Russell, M.A.W.E., is the mother of two adult children and lives in Ashland, Kentucky. She married her soulmate, David, after 21 years of singleness. Hobbies include walking, crocheting and taking mission trips to other countries. She has a B.A. from W. Va. Wesleyan College and an M.A. in World Missions and Evangelism from Asbury Theological Seminary.

Judge Kristin Ruth graduated from Campbell University in North Carolina and practiced law until she was elected to the bench in 1998. She has traveled world-wide on mission trips, and was recently named the 2003 American Business Woman of the Year. Kristin and Preston Ruth have one son, Kenan.

Mark Sanborn is known internationally as the high content speaker who motivates. He is the president of Sanborn & Associates, Inc., an idea lab dedicated to developing leaders in business and life. He is the author of numerous books and training resources. For more information, visit www.marksanborn.com.

Jessica Leigh Scales is a 15-year-old high school student who enjoys expressing herself artistically. She is a member of her school's Drama Club, The Service Club and the Conflict Resolution Group. She intends to work with special needs children as an adult and has logged many hours tutoring elementary school students.

Sylvia Gay Scott – artist of clay and pen – remarks on life as the best gift ever received. To be able to see the colors of splendor in everyday life through the love of family and friends helps her achieve all. Making Raleigh, NC her home, writing is her peace maker; sculpting soothes the soul.

Known as the Inside-Out Coach, **Jeanne Sharbuno** is a speaker, workshop leader, and certified professional coach through the International Coach Federation. She works with people in making career and life choices, and with individuals and organizations worldwide. An avid ballroom dancer, Jeanne lives in Atlanta, Georgia. Contact Jeanne at 678-443-4037 or Jeanne@mindspring.com.

Carol Spielvogel, born in the Maritimes of Canada, received a degree in Religion and Philosophy at Barton College in North Carolina. She has now returned to Canada with her husband, and lives lakeside near St. Margaret's Bay in Nova Scotia. She presently spends her time doing numerous crafts, decorating and "life studies."

Sarah Starr is the Director of Funding and Research Development at the Ohio State University Research Foundation, where she spends her time helping to find research funding. She is a Stephen Leader and Stephen Minister. In addition to writing, she also enjoys gardening, cooking, bicycling, walking and water aerobics.

Tammy Summers, M.Ed., LPC, NCC, is a licensed professional counselor in private practice working with individuals, families, couples and groups for almost 19 years. Her specialties include the treatment of eating disorders, panic disorder, depression/anxiety, grief and loss, family of origin issues, and divorce and separation. Contact Tammy at 919-844-2921 or Taslpc@aol.com.

Ana Tampanna facilitates insight and community by designing experiential activities to help women connect from the heart regarding key issues. Her book, *The Womanly Art of Alligator Wrestling: Inspirational Stories for Outrageous Women Who Survive by Their Wisdom and Wit*, highlights her involvement with friends and family, her experiences with cancer, and many other women's issues. www.alligatorqueen.com.

Dan Thurmon's unique speaking style, Speaking With Visual Impact,, incorporates world-class demonstrations of acrobatics and juggling as anchors to Dan's powerful learning points, creating unforgettable experiences for corporate and association audiences. He presently lives in Atlanta, GA, with his wife, Sheilia and children, Eddie and Maggie. Contact Dan at 770-982-2664 or www.danthurmon.com.

Robert Vanderberry, MD is a pediatrician and Addiction Medicine specialist who resides in Raleigh, North Carolina. Since 1980, his efforts have been directed at substance abuse prevention and treatment. His recent novel, *Professional Discourtesy,* deals with addiction, and can be purchased at www.vberrybooks.com.

Jodie Vesey is an etiquette expert and professional speaker. Her topics cover corporate etiquette, business attire and communication. You can contact Jodie at jodie@jodiespeaks.com or check out her web site at www.jodiespeaks.com.

Audrey Williams is a training manager at an electric utility association and an honors graduate of Fayetteville State University. She thrives on harmonious relationships and often acknowledges the blessing of genuine friendships. Audrey is an active church member who enjoys redecorating, collecting lighthouses, and observing scenery along country roads.

Ann Wright has over 20 years of management experience, and bachelor and master degrees in business leadership from Upper Iowa University. She works with individuals on their personal and professional development in a variety of areas. She lives in Iowa with her husband, Doug, and son Noah. Contact Ann at wrightsolutions@juno.com.